ℓ5

the Dublin Review

number twenty-nine | WINTER 2007–8

GW00482837

EDITOR: BRENDAN BARRINGTON

PUBLISHING ASSISTANT: ANGELINA LYNCH

The Dublin Review, number twenty-nine (Winter 2007–8). Design by Atelier (David Smith). Printed by Betaprint, Dublin.

ISBN 978 1 84351 112 0
ISSN 1393-998X

The Dublin Review is published quarterly. Editorial and business correspondence to *The Dublin Review*, P.O. Box 7948, Dublin 1, Ireland, or to brendan_barrington@yahoo.com, or faxed to +353-1-6788627. Unsolicited material should take the form of printed typescript only and should be submitted by post. If you wish to receive notification in the event that your work is not accepted, or if you wish to have the manuscript returned, please enclose an appropriately sized self-addressed stamped envelope or, if you live outside the Republic of Ireland, a self-addressed envelope with an adequate number of International Reply coupons. In the absence of a self-addressed envelope carrying adequate postage we will not be in contact with you unless we wish to publish the work. *The Dublin Review* assumes no responsibility for unsolicited material.

Visit our website: www.thedublinreview.com

SUBSCRIPTIONS: €30 / UK£24 per year (Ireland and Great Britain), €45 / US$50 per year (rest of world). Institutions add €12.70 / UK£10 / US$15. To subscribe or to order back issues, please send address and cheque or Visa/MC data to Subscriptions, The Dublin Review, P.O. Box 7948, Dublin 1, Ireland. Credit-card orders are billed at the euro price. Please indicate if credit-card billing address differs from mailing address. Alternatively, you may subscribe using the secure-ordering facility on our website, at www.thedublinreview.com.

TRADE SALES: *The Dublin Review* is distributed to the trade by Gill & Macmillan Distribution, Hume Avenue, Park West, Dublin 12. Sales representation: Robert Towers, 2 The Crescent, Monkstown, Co. Dublin, tel 01 2806532, fax 01 2806020.

The Dublin Review receives financial assistance from the Arts Council.

Contents | *number twenty-nine* | WINTER 2007–8

CORRECTION: *In the last issue, writing about the flooding in Hull, David Wheatley wrote: 'Also among the East Riding villages to flood was the appropriately named Burtwick, though long-time butt of adolescent jokes Wetwang remained above water.' The appropriately named village is of course Burstwick.*

Very important man

BRIAN DILLON

Friday 7 September

I'm on a flight from Prague to Istanbul, the second leg of a journey that started seven hours ago at Heathrow, trying to read a book about the history of human gesture, while being repeatedly elbowed in the ribs by my neighbour. It's close to midnight, and even allowing for the two-hour time difference between the UK and Turkey it's been a long day, and I can do without this panicked, muttering character and his flailing efforts to get comfortable. The food pacified him for all of five minutes and now he's at it again with the elbow. Interestingly, my book says that gesture has often been considered a sort of universal language, and I wonder if it's worth showing my friend here the pages devoted to various sorts of manual warnings and wardings-off: the raised palm, and worse.

Actually, I have no reason to feel so harried. Not only have I not paid for this flight, but I'm about to be put up for three nights in central Istanbul, just so that I can deliver a half-hour lecture on Saturday evening. The gig arose from a short essay on the subject of Victorian public-speaking manuals (more of these later) that I've recently published in *Cabinet*, a Brooklyn-based art and culture magazine of which I'm UK editor. This latter position has lately, thanks to the magazine's peculiar cachet in the art world (of which also more below), landed me a number of expenses-paid lecture slots. As the plane banks over the Bosphorus, into a spectacular electrical storm, and my neighbour settles down (he may just have gone rigid with fear), I'm starting to feel quite the pampered public intellectual.

At Atatürk airport it's raining so hard they can't take the luggage off the plane, and it's well after one in the morning by the time I clear arrivals and fetch up at an ATM, which promptly swallows my debit card. There's a courtesy phone beside the machine and the woman on the other end quickly cancels my card, but not before I get the distinct impression she's been cheerfully cancelling cards all night as they disappear into this very machine. I'm stunned by the humidity, sweating like a madman and not feeling very pampered at all. I dig out the one credit card whose PIN I think I remember and go looking for another ATM. As my cash flops out I'm joined by a middle-aged man whose night-shift-creased face is so unmistakably that of a massively-overpriced-taxi/shuttle-bus scam artist that I all but embrace him, being by now far too tired to go looking for the bona fide taxi rank and quite willing to be comprehensively fleeced if that's what it takes to get me into town. I let him steer me into a lift, assure him on the way down that yes, Ireland is indeed exceptionally green, and get bundled into a people-carrier bound for the Marmara Pera hotel.

In my room, I order a club sandwich and a beer, which seems the sort of thing that people who get flown round the world to do very little might order, when they arrive at their hotels, in the middle of the night, feeling tired and important. I phone F. and read her the motto printed on all the Marmara Pera's literature: 'Living well is the best revenge.' For what?

Saturday 8 September

A vast archipelago of talks and symposia surrounds the sale and exhibition of art these days: events mostly organized by museums, galleries, art fairs or the biennials that it seems no city can do without now if it wants to pass for culturally clued-in. Of these latter, the Venice Biennale, first held in 1895, is the most famous, but Berlin, Athens and Istanbul are all now on the European art-world calendar, along with Documenta (at Kassel every five years) and

Sculpture Projects Münster (every ten). This year, the happy conjunction of Venice, Kassel and Münster meant that people spoke, ironically at first, of doing the Grand Tour; as the summer wore on, the irony seemed to wane.

All of this art generates an awful lot of talk. Some of it is about the art but much of it, it seems, is supposed to make up for the art, or at least for a sense that the art at such exhibitions, fairs and festivals has been reduced to mere commodity status, or inflated into pure entertainment. A few years ago, as the Iraq War got under way, the chat was all about art and politics, but the subject seems recently to have shifted to the relationship between art and education, or the idea of art as education and education as art. Artists, critics and curators have been staging what I suppose forty years ago people called teach-ins; today the label is 'relational aesthetics'. You can't move for marathon lecture series, one-day ad hoc 'universities' and art installations that take the form of libraries, reading rooms or intellectual salons.

Hence my three nights in Istanbul. The Biennial has just begun, and with it a constellation of ancillary events of which mine is one of the more obscure. So obscure that I'm having trouble working out exactly what it's called. Anselm Franke, the Berlin-based curator who invited me, is calling it a 'Black Market for Useful and Non-useful Knowledge', but it's advertised on the Biennial website as a 'Mood Salon' and it seems also to be part of something called 'Floating Territories': a programme of performances, installations and debates taking places on a boat travelling between Istanbul, Athens and Venice. The evening involves a number of 'experts', seated at tables, each imparting their knowledge to one person, seated opposite, at a time. The theme for the event is 'atmospheric politics' – 'we understand "atmospheric politics" as the politics of the background, the politics of moods, gestures and mediality', says the publicity material.

I've elected to talk about Victorian gesture manuals: eccentric but apparently popular volumes aimed at aspirant public speakers, full of highly entertaining illustrations of frock-coated orators sawing the air and casting imploring looks toward the heavens. The most influential of these books was *Chironomia: or a Treatise on Rhetorical Delivery*, published in Dublin in 1806 by the Rev. Gilbert Austin, who elaborates a frighteningly complex system of bodily mapping, based on an abstract sphere, also illustrated, that surrounds the speaker.

The venue is a bar on a narrow street not far from the hotel. On the fourth floor, I'm greeted by the affable Anselm Franke and a contingent of very tall women from the Evens Foundation, a charitable organization in Antwerp that seems to be funding the whole thing. Anselm tells me I'm on twice, at 6.30 and 7.30. I grab a beer, wander out on a balcony to watch the sun sinking over the gleaming western districts of the city, and then follow my fellow experts upstairs to a tiny conservatory-like space in which four tables and eight chairs are neatly arrayed.

My neighbour is Dieter Roelstraete, curator of the Museum of Contemporary Art in Antwerp, who tells me he's just written a substantial catalogue essay on the theme of gesture, so I'm immediately anxious that my actually rather thinly-researched musings might not cut it in such company. Then my first interlocutor, Monika Szewczyk, turns out to be Dieter's partner, so I'm doubly worried. Monika is also a curator, currently based in Vancouver and about to move to Brussels. I launch into my lecture, showing her copies of Gilbert's illustrations and sketching out his system. Before long, she's explaining various contemporary theories of gesture and recommending books, which I suppose means the 'Mood Salon' business is working, because my 'expertise' has gone out the window and we seem to be having a conversation. Anselm appears and rings a tiny bell to tell us that time is up. I take a break, and swap email addresses with Monika and Dieter before my next client shows up. Ronny Heinemans is an artist, also living in Brussels. I tell him I live in Canterbury and he says he spent two summers, as a teenager, learning English in Ramsgate, not far away, and being chased by local boys for so much as looking at local girls. He listens patiently, then tells me – I'm embarrassed to have missed this – that Iraqis keep getting killed because the extended hand and raised palm that US soldiers use to ward them away is in their gestural lexicon a signal to approach.

It's all over after an hour and a half, and 'experts', 'clients' and assorted international artist-curator-critic types gather at the bar. It's been a distinctly odd experience – like a sort of intellectual speed-dating – and I'm not exactly sure what impression I've made.

Denise Robinson, a curator from London, introduces herself. We've spoken on the phone before. She's done the Grand Tour (she pronounces it with the proper irony) and is somewhat appalled by the shallowness of debate surrounding the big biennials. She bemoans the tendency to parachute in some intellectual celebrity to comment on the proceedings from what invariably turns out to be a debilitating theoretical distance from the actual art. Philosophers such as Slavoj Zizek, Alain Badiou and Jacques Rancière are the worst culprits, she says: all brilliant, all totally out of touch with what goes on in contemporary art galleries. I remind Denise that it was I who invited Rancière to the Frieze Art Fair in London two years ago, and interviewed him onstage on the subject of 'Aesthetics and Politics': which appearance has subsequently been mentioned in the pages of heavyweight art magazines like *Artforum* as a shorthand for all that's easy and flip about the art world's relationship with ideas in general and philosophy in particular. So it's all your fault, says Denise. Yes it is, I say, though I'm sure it's not.

I meet Alex Sainsbury, who is about to open a gallery in Spitalfields, London: a non-profit space, he explains, privately funded but non-commercial. He's wondering what to call it. Facetiously, I suggest he put his own name to it – open a gallery named after a supermarket chain – then it dawns on me that he is *an actual Sainsbury*, and there are already several cultural institutions in Britain with his family's name attached. Mercifully, at that moment I'm accosted by an Italian artist, Alex Cecchetti, who edits a magazine called *The Unready*, which exists only in fragments, as a temporary parasite in the pages of other publications. He'd like *Cabinet* to run a few pages, upside-down. By this stage, word has got around that I'm attached to *Cabinet*, and although I can take scarcely any responsibility for its skewed perspective on art, culture, science and everything under the sun, I'm soon out on the balcony being introduced to more artists and writers and German curators in austere spectacles, all of whom seem to be subscribers.

And then, weirdly, the evening ends. Or mine does anyway. I have some sort of catastrophic failure of social nerve and blow my whole burgeoning art-critic-cum-essayist cool in five minutes flat. Everybody out on the balcony is planning to attend the opening of a new gallery in a renovated hydroelectric power station just outside the city. It's half an hour's taxi ride away. For no good reason that I can think of – other, perhaps, than that despite all the engaging art talk and my fourth beer and the fact that I can smoke on the balcony (and I've decided that this being Turkey, where everybody smokes, I may as well smoke too), I still don't feel part of this scene, and anyway I'm in Istanbul, of all places, and I have no idea how or when I'm going to get back from said power station, and also I just seem suddenly sort of afraid of all of the above – I decline the invitation and claim to be too tired. It's a lie, and I'm regretting it even as I hit the street and realize it's only nine o'clock and I have literally nothing to do in Istanbul for the rest of the night except wander back to my hotel and curse again the remnants of that shyness (is that even a thing, when you're 38?) that I keep thinking has gone for good.

Sunday 9 September

The Atatürk Cultural Centre (AKM) is a vast concrete box, fronted with glass and aluminium, that stands on the eastern side of Taksim Square. The square is a palimpsest of twentieth-century Turkish history, and an allegory for present attitudes to the secular state founded by Atatürk in 1923. At its centre stands the Independence Monument. To the north is a somewhat desolate public park that replaced a football stadium in 1940. Numerous minarets are visible from the square, including a small grey metal tower that looks more like a ramshackle space rocket. The south side is dominated by vast hotels. AKM was first built, as an opera house, in 1969; it burned down during a performance the following year. The replacement structure, completed in 1978, was given a slightly more expansive remit: its design included wide foyers in which exhibitions could be held. Still, today it remains mostly an opera house and concert hall, closed in the summer and even during the winter opera season, darkened and empty during the day. The building is currently the object of some controversy: the city authorities would like to demolish it and continue Taksim's advance toward another sort of Westernization, of which the Burger King frontage across the square is just the most visible sign.

AKM is also the main venue for the tenth Istanbul Biennial. It's mid-morning when I arrive. The building's plaza is scattered with young couples, dawdling smokers and a couple of old women doting on a one-eyed cat. Inside, the yellow livery of the Biennial decorates the main lobby, where I buy a ticket and ascend a spiral staircase to the exhibition. The theme of this section of the Biennial is first of all the building itself and secondly its wider significance for the city. Its title is 'Burn it or not?' Against the gleaming metallic tiles of the first-floor foyer are hung large-format photographs, taken in 2005, by the Austrian artist Markus Krottendorfer: they show interior views of Moscow's Hotel Rossija, since demolished. Most of the art on show here depicts similarly doomed structures: buildings that conjure a lost utopianism that mirrors the plight of AKM itself. A slow, elegant film by Nina Fischer and Maroan el Sani shows vacant portions of the old Bibliothèque Nationale in Paris. Daniel Faust's photographs of the UN building in New York depict fixtures and fittings that speak of an aesthetic internationalism that looks as dated as the institution itself, while Japanese photographer Tomoko Yoneda frames similarly ruinous-seeming civic spaces in Hungary and Estonia. The overall effect is dolorous in the extreme.

But it's the building itself, with its hushed precincts in which security guards are drinking tea and chatting or shamelessly dozing in the shadows, that is most intriguing. At least half the international art crowd that has drifted in since I arrived, some of them still hefting luggage, having just got off their planes, is paying more attention to the architecture than the art. I'm not alone in nervously edging away from the exhibition areas to examine defunct light fittings and dusty air-conditioning outlets, empty display cases and yellowing photographs of opera singers. AKM feels strangely adrift from the busy square outside, stuck in a dead dream of secular Modernism. Eventually, curiosity gets the better of me and I head downstairs to enquire of the Biennial staff whether it's possible to explore the roped-off corridors and storage areas, and maybe even the auditoria. It seems I'm not the first to ask, and a tetchy security guard is summoned to assure the young woman at the ticket desk, once more, that there is absolutely no question of my, or anybody else's, departing from the officially sanctioned route through the exhibition. Once he's out of earshot she smiles an apology and explains that the Biennial is fortunate to have been allowed to use the public exhibition areas: everything else is definitively closed and off-limits even to her and her colleagues.

I go back upstairs and sit for half an hour in the semi-darkness outside the main auditorium, watching local art students arrive clutching their bright yellow catalogues. Then I wander away to do the Istanbul tourist things, occasionally catching sight, standing in the queue for the Blue Mosque museum or photographing the Sunday-afternoon anglers lined up along the Galata Bridge, of art tourists clutching their Biennial carrier bags and looking slightly lost. In the evening, sitting outside a small restaurant off Istiklal Caddesi, the city's main shopping street, I get invited to the next table by a pair of very drunken men who turn out to be accountants from my hotel. We do our best with my lack of Turkish and their limited English till it comes to the question of what exactly I'm doing in Istanbul. How to explain 'Floating

Territories'? I say I'm here for the Biennial, and I'm a sort of writer, and we finally agree that I must be a critic. The younger and drunker, Ehmet, who has so far not ventured a word of English, is overcome by hilarity at this revelation, orders another round of drinks and raises his glass. 'Important man,' he roars. 'Very important man.'

Wednesday 10 October

It's autumn, so it must be the Frieze Art Fair. Of the major art-world events, Frieze is a comparative upstart. It was founded four years ago by Amanda Sharp and Matthew Slotover, publishers of the London-based art magazine *frieze*. Housed each year in a huge marquee in Regent's Park, and host to 150 international commercial galleries, each of which has its own stand staffed by well-groomed gallerists, it's quickly become an essential stopover for collectors and, this year, a kind of punctum to the European Grand Tour. Like the biennials, it includes an ambitious programme of lectures and panel discussions. It is also the kind of event where you are likely to brush against, say, Bianca Jagger, or at least her bodyguard. There are press photographers even in the toilets. Last year, at the centre of a large entourage, Kate Moss was conspicuously the only person in the whole non-smoking venue allowed to blithely light up.

Wednesday is Professional View day and then Opening Night. F. and I arrive at the tent around four o'clock. Outside, two straggling lines of well-dressed smokers snake away either side of the entrance. A long covered ramp, flanked by the Press Office, VIP desk and VIP Courtesy Car desk, takes us to the interior. I've written a few entries for this year's catalogue, so I'm blessed with a VIP pass and we head straight for the VIP Room. This does not exactly elevate us above the throng in the manner you might imagine: at this point, before the official opening, practically everybody here is a VIP and we are anyway, after four years of this, well aware that there are a few strata of VIP-dom above us: chilled echelons where VVIPs and even VVVIPs congregate unseen by the merely VI. In fact, I half suspect that the most important persons never even make it as far as the Fair itself, merely lending to the proceedings the halo or rumour of their presence in London.

For sure, the VIP Room is full of obviously well-heeled folk paying £8 for a glass of champagne and wolfing bagels and baguettes from the bar before the real action – that is to say, the free champagne when the opening party proper begins at six o'clock, which beneficence said prosperous-seeming VIPs will by no means spurn – begins. But the VIP Room is also dotted with slightly dishevelled-looking art critics. Actually, they (that is, we) are probably not all that dishevelled-looking – it's just that by comparison with the burnished glow coming off the average VIP, even a not-quite-top-flight VIP, we look distinctly shabby. Adrian Searle, art critic of the *Guardian*, sidles up, wincing slightly, baguette in hand: he's been here since eleven in the morning, when the press were allowed in, and has just filed his copy. He's not sure he can face the crowd outside again, never mind the numbing quantity of artworks, but feels he should, and ambles off. The *frieze* (as opposed to Frieze) crowd has colonized a table in the corner. F. and I say hello to assorted editors and interns, and everybody rolls their eyes at the hothouse trade-fair atmosphere of it all, and we all agree that this is no place to try and look at art, but at least we get to see people and that's something.

It's become a reflex response, this: the idea that a vast overheated tent in the middle of London is less than conducive to aesthetic contemplation. But we're determined to resist such in-crowd ennui, and head back out into the fray. Everybody is talking about, and many people pointing the way to, an installation by the American artist Richard Prince. Best known for his photographic appropriations of advertising images in the 1970s, Prince has concretized his response to commodities by exhibiting a souped-up 1970 Dodge Challenger. It sits, bright orange, on a dais. Leaning against the car is a very tall and very shapely woman in hot pants and a bikini top, grinning broadly. Every now and again somebody (always male) engages her in conversation. All weekend, in the interests of this essay, I keep thinking I ought to at least find out her name, but each time I pass by the car I fail to muster the confidence, fearing I'll look like another of those men who tried to chat up the Richard Prince woman – presumably, the artist has factored the likes of me into the work's meaning.

This sort of engagement with the audience, or at least with the idea of an audience, is much in evidence. At the stand of the New York gallery Gavin Brown's Enterprise, a flea market is selling assorted tat donated by artists, and Jeremy Deller is giving away a free poster, on which are printed, in Hebrew, the lyrics of the Kinks' 1969 single 'Victoria'. Nearby, the Chapman brothers are defacing the image of the Queen on punters' banknotes. A photograph by Thomas Struth, *Museo del Prado* – part of a series depicting museum spectators – shows a crowd looking half-reverent, half-distracted before Velazquez's *Las Meninas*.

At six o'clock, somewhat dazed, we give in to the social whirl. At one end of the tent, an expanse of white plastic tables and chairs, like an empty beach, is slowly filling up. Beyond is a sea of champagne flutes, empty at present, and a phalanx of black-clad waiting staff whose trays are also conspicuously empty. I spot the writer Michael Bracewell and his partner, the artist Linder Sterling, in the crowd, and we struggle towards them. Aghast at the slowly gathering throng – it's like Hitchcock's *The Birds*, says Michael – they are ready to flee, and bequeath us their chairs. By the time we sit down, the champagne glasses are half full and there's an air of mild panic about the crowd, with the less bashful already staring down the staff and threatening to snatch at the free drink before the trays start to circulate. F. and I sit still for as long as possible, till it becomes clear that one of us will have to forgo dignity and join the melée. When the moment comes, it's still astonishing: several hundred money-eyed invitees and less moneyed gallerists, journalists and art students charge towards the full trays, all decorum banished by hours spent among too many people and too much art: the Frieze Effect.

Later, in the taxi queue, we run into Anjalika Sagar, who is one half of an artist duo called the Otolith Group. She and her partner Kodwo Eshun, she tells us, boarded the Floating Territories boat at Athens, planning as their contribution a showing of some infrequently-screened documentary films by Chris Marker. The trip was a disaster. The passengers quickly split into two camps: artists and their curatorial or critical colleagues who were keen to show their work or talk about what they'd seen, and freeloading partygoers who disrupted the official programme. Fights broke out on board. Anjalika is scathing, and none too keen either, it seems, on the chaos of Frieze opening night. She hands me her card, and invites us to a party the following night. An 'Anti-Frieze' party.

Friday 12 October

F. and I have arranged to meet Michael and Linder for a late lunch at Tate Britain. He arrives first, affecting as ever a sort of elegant fluster, genially bemoaning the whole hectic charade of Frieze Week. Michael is, if not the best dressed person I know, at the very least the smartest. In his presence, I always feel as though I've committed some appalling gaffe in the cuff department. His look sits somewhere between late-period Malcolm McLaren and mid-career Bryan Ferry: that is to say, a supremely tasteful take on Traditional English Gent, with enough Art-School Hetero Dandy (Ironic Post-Punk Version) thrown in to make the whole seem expertly casual, studiedly insouciant. He has in fact just published a book about the art-school prehistory of Roxy Music, and is feeling nervous about reviews, which are likely this weekend. He's not so sure that either beer-stained rock hacks or mainstream reviewers will quite get a book about a pop group that stops dead before they release their first record.

Linder hurries into the Tate café soon after, tears streaming down her face, grinning and catching her breath. This is what exceptionally hard-earned and criminally belated success looks like: she's just had five works bought by Tate Britain and, to her surprise, they've already been hung. In 1977, Linder made a collage – a naked woman scalpelled from a porn magazine, with a clothes iron where her head should be – for the cover of the Buzzcocks single 'Orgasm Addict'. She was already a prime instigator of the Manchester punk scene and keen student of early photomontagists like John Heartfield and Hannah Höch. Since then, she's continued to make her unsettling art while first leading her post-punk band Ludus – notorious for a performance at the Haçienda club that involved Linder, in a dress hung with raw chicken, wearing a large black strap-on dildo – and latterly moving into performance art, in which capacity she has been known to dress as Clint Eastwood, cheroot and stubble and all. Today, she's unbearded, and elegantly amazed that her still shocking montages of female flesh and household appliances are hanging in the Tate, the second gallery she ever entered.

Linder and F. talk about the book that F. is writing, and the difficulty of finding time for Art and Thought when you've got a full-time job; but Michael and I, who have not had anything like full-time jobs in a long while, are getting twitchy. We're pre-gig. This evening, at the Photographers' Gallery, near Leicester Square, Cabinet is staging an evening of lectures: setting out its stall as purveyor of cultural miscellanea, historical and scientific curiosities, oblique artistic interventions. Michael is first up, talking about the seaside surrealism of Lancashire, where he and Linder live. I'm attempting more about the gesture business. But things have become complicated. Our brightest idea, our singularly brilliant contribution to the whole art-world educational-performative nexus, has been to have an actual working replica made of the gestural sphere from Gilbert Austin's Chironomia. It's not the first: a professor at Harvard in 1830 used a bamboo version to teach his students. We've persuaded Conrad

Shawcross, up-and-coming sculptor, to make the thing, out of steel. At a key moment in my presentation, the labelled sphere will descend over me, mapping my every gesture, and I'll continue my talk in strict accordance with the Rev. Austin's principles, to (we hope) general surprise and amusement. All week, we've been cracking wise, in *Cabinet* circles, about various *Spinal Tap* scenarios: my getting trapped inside, Conrad turning up with a sphere that's six inches wide instead of six feet, and so on.

I should be at the gallery. The Tube from Pimlico to Leicester Square feels like Atatürk airport, and I arrive in Great Newport Street flushed and nervous. But I can see Karen McQuaid, who runs the gallery's talks programme, through the glass door: she's been highly amused by our spherical ambitions. As I open the door, she gives me the iciest of looks. Gathered in the foyer is a silent, ashen party: editor-in-chief Sina Najafi and his *Cabinet* crew, various gallerists and a young man, drenched with sweat and holding an enormous pair of bolt cutters, who I assume is Conrad Shawcross, sculptor. At his feet is a neat pile of scrap metal. A narrative slowly forms. Conrad arrived in a van, bearing his sphere, and Atlased it into the foyer, scraping paint off a glass door in the process. Enter irate gallery manager, threatening a bill for £400. *Cabinet* people arrived, calmed everybody down. Then the sphere, which was indeed six feet wide, failed to fit through the next door, so Conrad cut it in half with the giant bolt cutters, intending to reassemble it for the performance. At which juncture the gallerists panicked: a vast metal object, now with jagged extremities, was starting to look like a Health and Safety matter. The eventual upshot: Conrad, now without transport for the sphere, was forced to destroy it on site. He was heard, Sina tells me later, muttering 'my sculpture, my sculpture…' as he hacked away. Everybody now feels very bad.

Michael, Linder and F. arrive, and somehow in the telling of the story of the sphere we get over it and the evening goes well. The point is to present a cabinet of curiosities in action: some examples of the more eccentric topics the magazine has lately addressed. Michael essays something like an ironic church-hall lecture, complete with slides, on the twin resorts of Morecambe and Heysham, which also turns out to be a condensed history of English attitudes to glamour, leisure, sea and sex. Maiken Umbach, a lecturer from the University of Manchester, talks about artificial volcanoes built by German aristocrats in the eighteenth century: she's brought with her a lump of basalt, which sits on the table in front of her, gleaming blackly, as she speaks. Sina invites volunteers from the audience to sample miracle fruit: a West African berry that makes whatever you eat next, however sour, taste deliciously sweet. I do my best, without the sphere, to demonstrate the strangeness of the Rev. Austin's lessons in gesture. This involves a not inconsiderable amount of flailing about onstage, trying to approximate the attitudes struck by Austin's diminutive orators. It seems to go down well.

Saturday 13 October

It's our last full day in London. At the Fair (F. having wisely decided to spend the rest of the day with friends and family), I try to counter the Frieze Effect by focusing only on photography. Before long, given the profusion of works, I've narrowed this down, rather absurdly, to square-format photographs. There's something, I reason, modest and self-contained, as well as old-fashioned, about that format. It still leaves me with a lot to look at. There are five photographs by Rinko Kawauchi, a young Japanse artist who specializes in washed-out but intimate studies of her family and daily life. The work would be merely diaristic were it not also on such a large scale, and so unsettling. The best of the five is a close-up of the gaping mouths of about twenty carp, thrusting themselves hungrily from the surface of a pool. I find a few works, too, by one of my favourite photographers: the German Candida Höfer, who exhibits vast prints, several feet square and extraordinarily detailed, of her images of architectural interiors. I stand for ages looking at a photograph of a

Renaissance altar, then back up and nearly step on the toes of a couple behind me, just as the woman is turning to the man and saying: 'I really like the big ones, don't you?'

At midday in the VIP room there's an air of general depletion. A deep queue has formed at the bar, but most of the people at the tables are looking shattered. Perhaps some of the most obviously wealthy are post-deal, or post-no-deal. I sit looking out at the park, where, apparently, people are having a perfectly normal Saturday afternoon, and only the occasional child or jogger pauses to peer at the haggard specimens within. Nearby, two young women are discussing the teaching skills and general demeanour of a prominent academic and curator. 'He's just a bit … coquettish,' sighs one. I turn to my notes on the art I've seen and the people I've met, here and in Istanbul, and realize there are few scenes I'd rather be vaguely attached to, every now and again, than one in which the sort of seriousness and passion with which these two students then go on to discuss the art around them is allowed, and encouraged. Even the air of ludicrous privilege outside among the potential buyers, even the atmosphere of jet-setting, floating-island detachment that makes me partly doubt the art-and-education enterprise, cannot quite diminish the creative energy of the whole unruly milieu: artists, writers, curators, collectors and colourful hangers-on. Then again, at the next table, at the centre of a group of Americans who seem to be organizing a party in Los Angeles to which they are wondering whether they ought to invite certain Hollywood stars, a man in a trucker hat is shouting into his phone. 'I want a girl playing Motown songs. In a gorilla costume.'

The scattering

JAKI McCARRICK

As he stood on the shore gazing at the sea, water began to seep through the eyeholes of his boots. He could feel the weight of the year that had been, and wished by wishing it would slip away from him into the tide.

The coast drew in by the green mobile home up on the cliff. He looked up at the big grasses swaying in the wind, at the wooden gate set into the cliff-steps, and at the curtains inside the home tied back neatly with bows. How he'd like to have lived by the sea in a caravan or a mobile home, he thought, kicking a gold stone out of the sand. He turned and walked in the direction of the cliff-face, saw the mile-long stretch to Whitestown, white and quiet, strewn with mounds of silky walnut-coloured seaweed.

He thought of September, when they had stood on the end of Carlingford pier and scattered Gerry's ashes into the harbour. At first he had hated the idea, but Eva insisted it was what Gerry had wanted. Now, three months on, on the first day of the New Year, the thought that his brother was out there in the sea began to reassure him about the whole grisly business.

Beyond the heaps of seaweed he saw the skeletal remains of an old boat. He stepped into the hull, pulled at some rotting wood, and in the gap noticed two small bottles on a ledge: one, a white plastic Our Lady of Lourdes with a blue crown cap, and the other, brown and medicinal-looking, tied round the neck with coffee-coloured string. Turning the brown bottle in his hand, he guessed it had contained a tincture for wounds, though it had no odour, except of salt.

Further along the beach he saw a car parked above the dunes. A woman was standing by the edge of the dunes looking at the sea. She was holding a blue plastic bag tensely against her cream coat. He thought of turning back as he was now alone on this stretch and did not want to alarm the woman, who had begun her descent to the beach. Suddenly a dog came bounding towards him. He had seen the exuberant three-legged collie on the beach many times, always alone, absurdly oblivious to its missing limb. When it ran towards her the woman shooed it, and it carried on in the direction of Carlingford.

As he passed the woman he said hello, but she ignored him. She was familiar. He turned and watched her stop at the boat, but could not place where he had seen her before. He walked on.

Everyone had been quiet on the pier. (Even when his father had nearly fallen into the water at his turn to scatter.) They had been led by Eva along the beach rather than the pier road, and he had raged at the sight of all these people made traipse in the dusk across stinking lobster cages, stones and dark-green pools. There they were, this mass of family and friends, stepping over stones and pools – children, women in heels – to scatter Gerry's ashes, and, miraculously, the whole thing had gone off in fine style. A blazing pink sun had come out on a day filled with rain; the muddy shore to the steps of the high-walled pier was thronged with chattering sandpipers; the evening light curled around the edge of the Mournes onto the flat black stones of the harbour beach.

He rested the shells and stones he had collected on a tuft of sandy grass and, sitting on a rock, wondered if he should leave a note. What would he say? That he had slipped out of the scheme of things? That he had looked at his life after Gerry had died and found it a frightful mess: his job, his marriage, his house, his own self? That only a few moments of his existence here and there had truly belonged to him: last year's visit to Belfast, Aisha, the black-haired Polish girl, the hotel she'd brought him to, the one night of clarity? He checked his pockets: no pen or paper. He thought he heard Gerry speak his famous aphorism, *Never waste a journey*. At first it registered as a taunt for his lack of preparedness with the note, then as a kind of plea.

The whitish light over the sea had given way to a dark anvil-shaped cloud moving in from the north. He thought of his wife and the length of time they'd been married. Here, in the bracing air, he could honestly admit the years were only a number to him – he could easily walk away. Then why hadn't he? Instead, he went round in a state of permanent uncertainty. And this being so, Gerry's aphorism gave his quickly mounting doubts about walking into the cold sea something to cling to.

As he came off the beach at Templetown and headed for his car, he noticed on the side of the road a small shrine. There was a bright red poinsettia (with a blue plastic bag skirting the pot) on the ground in front of a low marble-engraved stone, together with coloured beads, dead flowers, holy medals. The stone read: *To our mother, Jean McConville, murdered by the IRA in 1979 and believed buried on this beach.* He looked up at the big signpost for Templetown advertising its recently acquired blue-flag status. A blue flag for a clean beach. The people of the Peninsula had worked hard for it; he'd seen them on Sundays lugging rusty beds with loose springs from the rocks under the dunes, plucking canisters of farming chemicals from the shore. They had made this beach, once so full of waste and death, clean and safe. They – and the industrious tide, which was like forgiveness and made everything new.

After shaking the sand from his boots he opened the car door then stopped to stare again at the sea. He had left the house, a few miles into the hills, to buy cigarettes for his wife. He'd have to hurry now to Lily Finnegan's who would shut her pub early on New Year's day. But he was unable to rush. He slipped into the car and drove towards Lily's, thinking about Gerry out there in the darkening sea, far beyond his reach – and Aisha in Belfast who wasn't.

A drink on one's own

GREG BAXTER

Whenever I cover stories outside the office, I like to procrastinate in the city. Other journalists hail taxis while jotting down notes on their notes, or jog back to their computers while the memories are still fresh, but I take circuitous walks through the centre, window-shop, browse bookstores. In April – it might have been May – I sat through a four-hour conference on healthcare in the Conrad Hotel. I had been out very late the previous night, so I hid in the back rows unshaven and smelling of sweet cheese and nicotine and sent texts to all the people I'd been with to blame them for my hangover. Now and again I'd write down something that was said by a man addressing the crowded room. He would say something like: The more money *I* make, the better patients feel. And everyone would clap like seals at a zoo.

I skipped the free lunch, roast chicken – who would I sit with, and what would I talk about? – and made my way through Stephen's Green. The morning had been bright and warm, but by now the day had come down cold and soapy, and it was beginning to rain. A few black umbrellas emerged from and disappeared into the trees. The rain was falling softly into the treetops and loudly into the little ponds. My bag was heavy. I had crammed in eight books that morning – I never know what mood I will be in – assuming the weather would hold and I could grab a little sunlit patch of grass and read for an hour or two. But I was happier this way. For my first couple of years in Ireland, the rain depressed me. Now whenever it is warm and agreeable, I lie around dreaming of grey skies and wind and short days in December.

I stopped into McDaid's – a regular spot for me – and sat on a stool in the window, where I could watch the rain intensify and bash the little alleyway between the Westbury and Bruxelles. The glass was still fogged at the four corners. Nobody knew then that we were headed for the rainiest summer in a hundred years. I ordered a pint of Guinness. I drink Guinness only when I want to avoid becoming unreasonably drunk.

There was one man at the bar, a big black man in a Nike tracksuit and bling sunglasses – surely a Westbury resident – and a white-haired couple at one of the small tables in the very back. The television – above the front door and completely out of my sight – was showing rugby, a repeat from the southern hemisphere, and only the bartender, who looked very much like Anthony Perkins in *Psycho*, but shorter, with a more pronounced chin, was watching, and only then from time to time. The black man, an American, drank a gin and tonic and said things about the music industry – who was who in New York, L.A., etc., and old stories about people he considered legends. The bartender, the only person to whom he could possibly have been speaking, agreed in nods but had nothing to add. Two German girls came in and sat at the short side of the bar, their backs directly to mine, and when the cold blew in the black man said, Merry Christmas, motherfucker! to no one in particular.

Outside, tourists in bright jackets and hoods stopped to consider McDaid's and Bruxelles, wondering if they were restaurants, if they might find some Irish stew and soda bread. The tourist will not accept anything less than the confirmation of his prejudice. The tourist believes he and his notion of the world are *desired* – this is the very idea that drives him to faraway places. It is his obligation to turn locals into foreigners. He is always jolly, whether he loves or hates the unfamiliar. And at night, in his hotel room, reading the book he bought to keep him company, or writing in his little diary, or just staring out the window, he retunes the instruments of his encounters to play music that he understands.

I placed my books on the ledge in front of the window. I had Mansfield and Hemingway, because later on I'd be talking about them with my creative writing students; a book by William Saroyan, a gift from a student that I always carry with me; and Gogol – I had just taught 'The Overcoat' and was thinking about teaching 'A Diary of a Madman'. I also had some short stories by Melville, Breton's *Manifestoes of Surrealism*, Ian McEwan's *First Love, Last Rites*, and *Literary Occasions* by V.S. Naipaul. My pint came. It was a cold glass and the head had spilled over the sides, and it was pleasant to behold. I took a sip immediately.

The journalist by his nature is a parasite. Whether he does good or harm on this earth – whether he, as Mencken describes, thumbs his nose at dignitaries or acts like them – his *nature* is to eat at somebody else's table. There is no point insulting him. If this is a man's nature, what else can he do? Of all the occupations in which a parasite can find happiness, journalism is surely the most noble.

And it saved me from ruin. When I moved to Dublin from Louisiana, I was twenty-nine and broke, with three degrees and three years' experience as an editorial assistant. I wanted out of the States – my job had finished when I got my degree, and all I could find to pay bills was a webmaster gig at a local TV news station. I spent my last six months in Baton Rouge drunk. I blew my savings, wrecked two cars, and got into serious trouble with women. Seven months after I showed up in Dublin, still unemployed, with credit card debt I could not possibly pay back, somebody finally offered me steady money, and I took it: thirty-year-old cub reporter for a weekly medical newspaper, not one day of experience. I was given a phone and a stack of papers with no explanation. I thought I'd been hired as a sub-editor, since that was all I knew. I asked, in a roundabout way, how to be a reporter. The news editor told me to telephone people and *get the story*. It was no good telling them all I was a novelist. I started making calls, but I wasn't very good. I wrote everything backwards, and forgot to ask all the important questions. But the news editor was patient: at least I was prolific. I'd write about fifteen stories and briefs every day, working through my stack. After a while, under generous tutelage, I improved. I started travelling to healthcare conferences and sitting down with influential people. My book of contacts began to expand. I found myself chasing hostile subjects down corridors. I was asked to do radio interviews about big stories and was surprised to find that I – the struggling American author in exile – had an embarrassingly huge amount of knowledge about the Irish health service.

I opened the Mansfield and the Hemingway. I teach 'Daughters of the Late Colonel' and, depending on my mood, any number of Hemingway stories – that evening I'd be teaching 'A Clean, Well-Lighted Place'. I took my notebook out in order to write a few things I wanted to say about them. But this seemed to desecrate the calm of the moment so I decided to write nothing.

I turned to find the black guy staring at me. He said something like, Shit, how many books are you reading?

I moved so he could see them better.

That's a lot of motherfucking reading. You teach?

Yeah, I said.

All fucking right, he said – I remember he said that. He went back to his gin and tonic. He had nothing with him. No reading. No phone. He just seemed to want to stir his straw and now and again take a drink, but not get drunk. I waited a moment and went back to my pint.

If I had been a faster walker, I might never have landed the teaching job. I was almost out the door of the Irish Writers' Centre. I was putting my headphones back in, wishing my skin away. It was October, 2006.

I had turned thirty-two in August, and had, four months before that, been passed over for promotion to news editor at the paper. I was partly relieved at this – it reaffirmed my sense that I was not perceived as serious or happy. I had laboured over the decision to apply, because I thought I was a shoo-in (I had become an excellent medical journalist), and I knew it would change everything. I would have to stop forgetting the healthcare industry every day at 5.30 – I'd have to strategize, always be one step ahead of the news. I would also have to reassess my hopes in life, or defer them. When I was interviewed for the position I told nauseating lies about my ambition as a journalist. I really laid it on thick. Turns out I never had much of a chance. The job was given to the editor of a competing paper – a nice guy who liked to talk and shorten people's names (overnight, Dylan became Dyl, Colin became Col, Holly became Hol). My productivity dropped off instantly. At first it might have been some disappointment that I was less respected than I thought, but that didn't last long. I didn't dislike the new guy. On the contrary, he was one of the friendliest and most imperturbable people I'd ever worked with. I simply couldn't drum up any stories.

One day, in a meeting, I asked the news editor to pass me along some more press releases, so that I could increase my output. I was desperate. He seemed surprised. He said something like: I don't want to distract you from your own stories. I was like, *What* stories? I probably knew it always, but that was confirmation: I had no initiative; journalism was not in me. The first news editor had been a mentor. He had pushed me, and anybody with a brain cell can respond to that. The new guy, at his own peril, had simply tried to show respect.

I knew I had to go, but Ireland is not like America. You can't just fill your CV with bullshit job titles and switch careers when you feel like it. In Ireland, I was a journalist, whether I liked it or not. PR, the lone alternative, was unthinkable. I could have quit the newspaper and freelanced, but giving up the job you hate to do the same thing, except at unsociable hours and for less pay, is just panic. I had also conceded my failure as a novelist. I was either no good, or I was extremely good, but either way I was not writing books anyone wanted to publish. I was, at long last, nowhere.

I found the website for the Irish Writers' Centre in a halfhearted search for any organization that gave money to writers; and there I came across the ad: *Tutors wanted*. This was the kind of job I'd always wanted: no boss, no abstract performance targets, no HR, no corporate lexicon to spice up the day-to-day routines of running a business. Moreover, having taught creative writing for a year at Louisiana State University, it was paid work I felt I might be naturally good at.

I knew only two people in Ireland with any status in literary society (a phrase that quivers at the back of my throat). One was an old boss of mine, the publisher at Lilliput Press, Antony Farrell (I have not mentioned that I lived in Ireland for a year in 1997 and worked at Lilliput, because that is a whole other story). I find it physically difficult to ask people for help. I agonize over it. I become nauseated and, I mean this seriously, have suicidal thoughts. I hate it, probably, because most writers I have met do it for a living. And I have watched a great many buffoons ascend mightily, and I have despised their mediocre brains and envied their success. They revealed the duplicity in me – a duplicity that is gone now – that was my deepest secret. I wanted what they had, but not the way they got it.

Antony got into publishing, I believe, for two reasons only: to maintain a market for really good writing (he published the essayist Hubert Butler, for whom the phrase *really good* is helpless understatement) and to throw parties. It is slightly easier to ask for help from people you respect, and I knew connections were invaluable when looking for jobs in Ireland – it was how I got my interview at the newspaper, and arguably why they hired a guy with no experience. I asked Antony if he knew anyone at the Centre, and could he give me a recommendation. He said he knew the director, Cathal McCabe, and suggested he introduce us at the launch of some book, by some writer, on that evening in October. Antony prefers to handle all such business informally, preferably in the milieu of carnival, because he is unimpeachable there – usually in bright red trousers.

I remember that it had been very clear but not too cold that night. I was suffering from nerves and did not eat lunch. I had my teaching experience, but it was pretty flimsy, and I had nothing but magazine publications to my name. I killed an hour just walking, wondering what I'd say on behalf of myself, why I deserved to tell anybody if they could or could not write, and when I arrived the reading room was full of people drinking white wine and nodding – everybody, as I feared, seemed to know each other. I spotted

Antony. Anyone who has ever met Antony knows that he does not so much mingle as *introduce*. I was handed off at once to the new editorial assistant, presumably because we had that job in common. I didn't want to mingle. I only wanted to shake hands with Cathal, tell him I'd sent my CV a few days before, and get out. Antony had forgotten why I'd come, and I felt extremely clumsy for imagining that my predicament had weighed on a man who had bigger concerns. I felt suddenly and profoundly impertinent – like I always do when seeking favours.

The launch was in full swing. I asked if Cathal were there and Antony said he thought so but wasn't sure, that he was a tall man with a northern accent. I stood by myself in the middle of the room and finished a glass of very bad wine. I started to make my way out. The stairs were crowded and a woman laughed as I walked past her. I felt as though I had witnessed my own execution. I was pushing through the doorway to the foyer, putting on my headphones – this was really how close it was – when I heard the accent. Perhaps, unconsciously, I had stopped to give it one last listen. In any case, I heard it. I considered leaving anyway. If Antony had forgotten, Cathal couldn't possibly know I'd come to say hello, and I'd just be annoying him. If I had not been working as a journalist, and become somewhat practised at approaching people who did not know me and may not want to talk, I would have simply retreated. But my inner voice – it emerges *very* rarely – told me not to waste the opportunity. I went up the stairs, found the man with the accent, asked if he was the man I sought – he was – and told him Antony suggested I say hello, that I had applied for a job as a tutor. Did I have experience? Yes. He said he'd take a look at my CV. I thanked him. Not long after, I got a phone call for an interview, which went well. I had never prepared for anything so much in my life. There was not much money in it, but I could teach as many nights a week as they wanted.

Resentment, if you let it, will weave itself into your DNA, and replicate. Every cell in your body becomes it. You feel nothing authentically, and you produce reactionary trash. You must let go of the desire to bring down the society you loathe. You must learn to discard any hope of making a difference. You must stop asking dumb questions.

Woolf: *I want to think quietly, calmly, spaciously, never to be interrupted, never to have to rise from my chair, to slip easily from one thing to another, without any sense of hostility, or obstacle.* Montaigne: *When I think of growing, it is in a lowly way, with a constrained and cowardly growth, strictly for myself.* And Henry Miller: *What I like about Dudley and some of the others is that they know enough not to want to do a stroke of honest work ... Sink or swim is their motto. They look at their fathers and grandfathers, all brilliant successes in the world of American flapdoodle. They prefer to be shit-heels, if they have to be.*

When I moved to Dublin, I simply transplanted myself. I woke every morning at dawn and put on three or four layers and a winter hat and bashed revisions into my first book. And when that failed I bashed a second book into existence. No thought I had was quiet. Everything was a military march. I could not imagine a fate of anonymity – life was meaningless without impact. I believed that I could alter society. I had sworn an allegiance to art. Whenever I referred to it, I used the word *we*. How pathetic that self seems to me now: *It is enough for me to hear someone talk sincerely about ideals, about the future, about philosophy, to hear him say 'we' with a certain inflection of assurance, to hear him invoke 'others' and regard himself as their interpeter – for me to consider him my enemy* [Cioran].

Months before I found work at the paper, I took on a contract job that was humiliating and paid nothing. I listened to taped speeches and phone conversations and transcribed them. Because I type with four fingers, and have no short-term memory (though my long-term memory is quite good), it took me hours to transcribe a few minutes' worth of tape. I had to rewind every few seconds. And my work was so mistake-riddled that I was invariably docked 20 per cent of my pay. It was mainly corporate work, and often the voices were inaudible. French accents (it was a French company). Bad tapes. Words I had never heard of. I was like Akaky Akakievich, just copying. The guy who served as a kind of boss was calling me every fifteen minutes asking how I was getting along. I told him I would be going a lot faster if he stopped calling me every fifteen minutes. He would laugh but he would call me fifteen minutes later. Apparently his other transcribers (though the title we all had was *journalist*) could type. In four months I probably made two hundred euro. I should have quit, but I needed the money – any amount was better than nothing. And I was writing my novel, which was going to be great, and revolutionize fiction, so I figured I had dignity. A man who believes in his own inviolability can withstand any cruelty, every form of humiliation imaginable.

By the time I gave up the desire to write books that would annihilate society – which was nothing more than the desire to write myself back into society – I had almost nothing left of myself. I wasn't a writer at all – just a slave to my own preoccupation with people who were published.

I got another pint. I felt unusually tipsy and wanted a cigarette. I had set my phone to silent but I could see that the screen was flashing. It was work. I needed to get moving soon.

All the successful journalists I know – who are my age or thereabouts – have one thing in common: they become excited by news, and when there is none of it, they are lost. When they have a story to write they rush to write it. Their hearts will explode if they don't. I, on the other hand, feel nothing but monotony. But after seven months of unemployment, living under a roof you're not paying for, fighting for television rights at the age of thirty, you capitulate to monotony. No matter how much you might loathe an honest day's work, no matter how little you want to be on phones or sitting through press conferences and writing down every infuriating detail of things that do not matter, you want that pay cheque. You want a drink or some new shoes, or some socks without holes in them. You want a little comfort. An iPod. Some new jeans. A holiday in Paris. A camera phone. A few extra sports or film channels. A dinner out. A bottle of wine that does not taste like vinegar. A steak you don't have to stew four hours to make tender. A means of transportation. Microsoft Word. A new winter coat.

After three years of working as a journalist, my life had become a junkyard of comforts. It must be true that to many – to all but a few – this junkyard is the meaning of life. Otherwise the fabric would collapse. If there were not people whose whole life was an Audi, or toilet-roll holders, or a television, or fancy lampshades, or an expensive birthday party for their four-year-old, civilization would end today, this minute.

Meanwhile, the writer who struggles to appease significance wanders the junkyard like a nomad, gathering artifacts, evidence of his greatness. Slowly he assembles a band, or joins one. I was at a wedding once in Tallahassee, Florida, where an acquaintance of mine – a writer named Adam – was getting married at the house of a well-known author. This author had won a Pulitzer Prize – a fact impressed on me by numerous guests, who asked several times, 'Would you like to see Bob's *Pewlitzer*?'

At the time of the wedding I had been working at the *Southern Review* for almost three years, and in that time we received, without fail, at least two manuscripts a week from Tallahassee, specifically from the creative writing programme at Florida State University, from which Adam had recently graduated, and where Bob was now teaching. A writer named Virgil Suarez, who was prolific without precedent, who at all times had *one thousand* submissions on the desks of editors, had been lecturing there a few years. Since this napalm-submission tactic worked for Virgil, it had become standard practice among MFA students there, whether or not they were prolific.

As expected, all the FSU culprits were in attendance at the wedding. Bob read a poem in Vietnamese. We stood on his front porch and he really bellowed that shit. I couldn't stop laughing. My eyes burned from trying to hold the laughter in. Some people around me were disgusted by my lack of awe –

in such proximity to a Pulitzer. They elbowed each other and nodded toward me.

For some reason it had seemed to Adam like a good idea to tell his fellow students at FSU that we – at the *Southern Review* – spent at least an hour each week having a great laugh at their expense: the stacks of submissions that plagued our office like locusts. Of course, a fight nearly broke out. The FSU guys formed a huddle. I didn't know, then, what Adam had said, so I just walked over and tried to make chitchat. I asked if there were any good places in town to drink. One said, Not dressed like that. I asked where a good place in town to eat was. One said, Try the Irish restaurant, you know, *McDonald's*. I asked, What's that supposed to mean? One said, I think it means *watch your back*. It would have escalated had I not been at the wedding of a guy I liked. I shrugged and left them alone.

My beer was finished. The black man was flirting with the German girls. My phone flashed again and I took the call. The news editor asked how the conference went. I said it went well. Anything front page? Oh, definitely. The rain was the same. I had no umbrella and no waterproof jacket, so the walk to the quays was going to be wet, and for the rest of the afternoon I'd be sitting in an uncomfortable puddle at my desk.

I put the books back into my bag and threw the bag over my shoulder – it seemed heavier now after two pints. The black guy gave me a nod. Earlier, the white-haired man from the back had walked out, rapping his knuckle on the bar as he went. Perhaps they had held a conversation earlier, or maybe they knew each other from the Westbury. Anyway, I had the feeling they didn't expect to see each other again. The black man told the white-haired man to take it easy. The white-haired man told him to do the same. The black guy said, Ain't nothing else *to* do.

I stepped out and stood in the rain. Why hurry when it would not make a difference? No matter what I did, I was going to get wet. I felt a mild sense of escape, in this foreign city, where the question of my writing was apropos of nothing, from the destiny I had coveted for the best part of a decade. I summoned the image of the future I was going to avoid: the author with old knees in his nightdress, creaking down the staircase in the middle of the night. He has woken his cat, who runs under his feet toward the kitchen. He goes into his study and turns a desk lamp on. He stands before a bookcase and squints at the shelf he has filled all by himself – books and journals, a medal, a certificate of some excellence. He reads his fine titles. One book in particular is opened and admired, but with ambivalence. He has read from them all over the world. They have earned him accolades and sex. One was translated into many languages. But what he and all his acquaintances knew but none would admit was this: each book was a diminution. Each year of his life was a failure. He sought to represent his age, a people, the place where he came from. To be recognized as genius or prophet. He never asked why it mattered. He was an expert in taxidermy: like the tourist and the journalist, he took reality, murdered it, stuffed it, and hung its head on a wall. And when the power to turn reality stale by contrivance ran dry and he was left with nothing but the wish to live forever, he learned that he was more *ordinary* than all men put together. Upstairs a student is asleep in his bed. She will leave him in a few months and go on to become an accountant with three children and never think of him again. He goes to the kitchen to feed his cat and have a glass of water. And he trembles while pouring from the purifier jug, imagining an afterlife.

As the man said

WILLIAM WALL

I would like to express my sympathy to the family on behalf of myself per-
sonally and the theme park company and the Ghost Train operator who is
gutted. Nothing like this has ever happened here in the last twenty years since
my company took over the running of the theme park. We are essentially a
property company and what we do is we rent space to rides to be operated on
site. The rides are all licensed by the appropriate licensing authority and we
have no involvement in that. All the rides at Happy Garden are fully compli-
ant with industry health and safety regulations but accidents do happen. If
you could cover everything there would be no need for regulations at all, but
you can't which is why we have health and safety, to prevent this kind of
thing. Which makes a something like this all the more upsetting for everyone
concerned and we would like to express our sympathy with the family of
Timothy Doran who was taken from us at so young an age, which is tragic
really. The Ghost Train operator is completely gutted. He is fully compliant
and is a member of the Showman's Guild in Britain and also has international
experience.

But all the experience in the world wouldn't prepare you for someone to
be decapitated in your ride. I'm saying decapitated but of course we have to
await the results of the post-mortem but I was one of the first on the scene
and I can tell you it was decapitation all right. I know you can't print that,
that's off the record now, but it was like a battlefield in there. Except of course
there is no evidence of any altercation I hasten to add. I'm talking about the
blood and the remains. The remains were like something out of *Terminator 3*. I
would like to express my sympathy in particular to Mr and Mrs Doran who I
know quite well. Frankie Doran was captain at the golf club there last year as

you know. My heart goes out to them and to all the family. We're all totally in shock.

As far as we can gather the incident took place in the Horror Cave section which has a narrow entrance which is essential because it is pitch black inside, and it looks like there was some leaning going on, that's off the record, I quote what our insurance rep said when he looked at it, but that's only a first-base position, we'll have to wait until the health and safety people make a full report. We're holding our hands up and saying let's wait until all the report is in and then we'll make a full statement.

At the moment we're in a state of shock as you can imagine. Especially as the little boy was handicapped, which we have a brilliant record on. All our rides are disability friendly and the whole site was revamped three years ago to comply with best practice internationally in the industry, ramps everywhere, full wheelchair accessibility, even though I know the wheelchair issue wasn't an issue on this occasion, but just to show that we've been responsive to the general area. Happy Garden are proud to say our record is second to none on disability issues. Which makes it all the more harder to take.

Mr and Mrs Doran are heroes around here for people like me, the way they fought tooth and nail for that little boy is nothing short of heroic. We were all behind them all the way. The people around here are the kind of people that get behind someone like that, we're the kind of people who are there when you need us. I don't have kids myself so I'm not well up on the school end of things but if you ask me it's a disgrace that someone like Tim Doran has to go away to a special school when all his mates are going to the local school, there should be provision for handicapped kids because let's face it it's hard on the other kids in the class, and of course the teachers, if you have someone disruptive who is handicapped and inclined to be disruptive through no fault of his own, which basically means the government is way off on this. I'm a member of the party myself locally as you all know well, but I'll hold my hands up and say that we're way off on this one and we should never have fought that case. You have to make provision full stop. Mr Doran who I know quite well personally, he was the captain in the golf club, was down here the time he was running for the Council and he was fully consulted on all the changes and as I understand it he personally took the Ghost Train ride at the time and enjoyed it. He was a big fan of the theme park; he told me he used to come here himself when he was a kid and he used to sneak down to the slot machines with the pocket-money when the mother wasn't looking, which, you know, a lot of local kids still do; it's amazing how these things carry on from generation to generation. Mr Doran was an excellent captain I will say that, and although he was elected as a single-issue candidate and effectively acted as a spoiler against our man and put him out for the first time in sixteen years, there's no hard feelings, that's politics and the electorate is the ultimate authority; but I have a feeling he'll be unseated again next time out. The party always wins in the long run and the single-issue candidate finds it very hard to keep the steam up going forward. We're already on a war footing now in the party, getting ready for the next round, but I'd say Mr Doran is still trying to find his feet.

Anyway, I digress, as the man said.

What I was going to say was, we used to have Timmy down here often with his brother. Now I can't say I knew him well only just to see him around. The Ghost Train operator knew him all right and I understand he has stated that he refused him entry on several occasions for health and safety reasons which I fully understand and which he is fully entitled to do; the legislation entitles him to refuse entry on health and safety grounds, which nobody is claiming was any kind of discrimination; this park is second to none on discrimination. Nobody has ever claimed against us not even coloured people. We have several coloured operators here, the bungee slingshot operator is Nigerian and we have several Lithuanians. Our policy on employing non-nationals is straight down the line, we make absolutely no distinction full stop. I would like to knock that on the head straight off. The Ghost Train operator was concerned for H&S reasons and the legislation entitles him to refuse entry on those grounds, which as it happens he was justified when you think about it. I mean if he stuck to his guns this time wouldn't we all be better off? But you never really hear about the successes which happen every day, when the health and safety checks and balances do what they're supposed to do, it's only just the one time that it doesn't work that you get in the papers and you people come out. But if you reported the good news stories all the time I suppose nobody would open the papers at all. But I would say frankly that the pressure on the Ghost Train operator was fairly intense to allow Timmy into the ride after the complaints and the pressure from the Council.

The ride was of course fully compliant as such and any normal person would have known not to lean out, in fact the Ghost Train operator always specifically mentioned that people should not lean out, or try to get out from under the safety bars, or try to exit the cars during the ride, or climb up on the cars, or try to make contact with the ghosts or in any way interfere with the smooth working of the ride, and there's a full notice to that effect, but, I suppose, you know, little Timmy was different to that, you know, and we'd be relying on his brother who accompanied him to restrain his actions, but I suppose it's a kind of a tribute to the ride itself that the brother was terrified, I mean that's what the Ghost Train ride is all about, isn't it?

So it looks like this is all just a tragic event that should never have happened.

I'd like to take this opportunity to express our sincere sympathy to the family of little Timmy Doran on behalf of myself and the company and the Ghost Train operator as such. I would like to also say that last year we ran a whole week when we had collection boxes at every ride in aid of the Society for Autism and this was in response to requests from Mr Doran. So we have been responsive to the general area and, as I already said, a few years ago we revamped everything for wheelchair accessibility. We would be holding our hands up here and saying it obviously wasn't perfect, but there's full transparency and accountability and we'll be making all our plans and specs available to the inspector. But I will say this, no company in the industry has done more for accessibility than Happy Garden. This theme park operates to the highest standards in the industry.

So allegations of negligence will be fought all the way, we don't accept negligence and we'll be making this plain through the court process going forward. We don't want to see this ending up in litigation that might take years and could work out badly for all concerned, and we'd like to extend our sincerest sympathy to the Doran family in this terrible time for them and to assure them of our fullest sympathy. All we ask is for Mr Doran to refrain from making unfounded allegations against the Ghost Train operator. We have a clean sheet as regards health and safety and needless to say we'd all prefer to have kept it that way, but Mr Doran's allegations are unhelpful at this time.

So we'd like to make the following statement re the unfounded allegations that have been circulating since yesterday: one, the train was travelling at the normal speed as specified and there is no way of altering the speed at the control box; two, the safety bar was in place and checked by the operator as usual and there is no way of lifting the bar while the ride is in progress; three, the ghosts do not interact in any way with the passengers, they only appear, make noises and gestures and disappear again, they have no remit to interact directly with anybody on the trains and if any ghost is found to have interacted this would be against company policy and will in no way be defended by the company; four, there was no misalignment of the track and further the company denies that any such alleged track misalignment would be sufficient to bring a passenger's head in contact with the scaffolding to which the outer wall of the ghost cave is attached; five, any alleged remarks made by the Ghost Train operator are hearsay and given the operator's vast international experience and his membership of the Showman's Guild unlikely to be proven, but should any remarks be proven to have been made in regard to poor little Timmy's mental problems this company will in no way stand over that; six, the company and the operator jointly and singly deny that the word freak was specifically used by anybody at any time in relation to the deceased, or that such words have ever been used in relation to anyone with mental or physical shortcomings by any of our operatives or other employees and that any allegation of such use of the word freak will be vigorously defended in court if need be; finally, the shouting heard by the other passengers is part and parcel of the Ghost Train experience which is to generate fear for a short period of time during the actual ride. The motto for the Ghost Train ride which is painted on the side is Max Fear and our Ghost Train is second to none in this regard. However our notice to passengers specifically warns anyone with heart problems not to get into the Ghost Train and we always advise passengers to read the full terms and conditions, and going forward we'll be updating this notice to take account of this tragic event in consultation with our legal people and the appropriate medical authorities.

But I will say this, some people don't understand fear. I'm not talking about specifically people with mental problems as such, it could be anybody. But we're not allowed to specify mental problems on a public notice. You'd never be able to put words on that one. I mean you can't say only normal people can go on the ride.

Fear is a natural part of our lives as you see every day now, passing through airports and so on. I'm winging it a bit here, but what I'm trying to say is little Timmy Doran was not able to fully partake in the fear like the rest of us and quite possibly he panicked unnecessarily and tried to get out. He might have easily thought the ghosts were the real deal, not seeing things the same way as the rest of us you know. As far as I understand the situation he would be what they call high-function which means he was not subnormal but the other way round to be honest. As far as I can gather at this point it's fair to say that shouting and the use of obscenity might be part of his condition and given that he might have thought the ghosts were really after him in some way he might have directed his obscenities at them rather than at the operator, which might also explain why he would have tried to exit the train in the course of the ride. Which would explain why the other passengers heard threats which they thought were directed at the operator even though they couldn't see anything in the dark. I will say the ghosts are completely shocked by the whole thing and a few of them are out sick today, which doesn't affect things anyway because the ride is closed for the duration.

So in the circumstances I think we should all take a rain check until the dust settles on this one. Nobody should be making unfounded allegations against anybody. In the meantime, the Ghost Train is closed until further notice but all the other rides in Happy Garden are operating as normal. As the man said, the show must go on. You can pick your free passes up at the office. Enjoy.

Strangers in the Capitol

EDNA LONGLEY

For once, the British question is a hotter ticket than the Irish question. As I write, in June 2007, three hundred years of Anglo-Scottish Union are being commemorated, execrated and debated. Before and after Alex Salmond's narrow victory in the Scottish parliamentary election, in the run-up to Gordon Brown taking over as prime minister, their different visions for Scotland focused attention on the wider state of the Union. To think about the UK as multinational is also to think about it as multicultural: an issue too often defined by political anxiety about British Muslims. Perhaps the various external and internal consequences of what the Victorian historian Sir John Seeley called 'the expansion of England' should enter the same reckoning. And even if England is now contracting, if Tom Nairn's thesis in *After Britain* (2000) holds then neither England nor its high-tide marks can return to any primal shore.

I want to examine two interlinked questions. First, how Protestant [unionist] Ulster sees England. Second, how England looks when Protestant Ulster – an approximate label like all the ethno-religious-national terms in this essay – is factored into the British question. On the first count, it might seem enough to say '*perfide Albion*'. Since the 1985 Anglo-Irish Agreement, many Ulster Protestants have seen London as eroding their own Britishness. (It took time for *British*-Irish to become the inter-governmental formula, no doubt because England and the Irish Republic are equally inclined to confuse 'England' with 'Britain'.) Yet even in 1912, when English poets such as Kipling and Swinburne backed Irish unionism, political appearances may have been deceptive. Discussing the (mild) Conservative response to Irish independence, John Turner argues that 'from the English Conservative point of view the national identity of non-English parts of the Union was always to be regarded instru-

mentally ... What had been an object of intense passion, because of the exi-
gencies of English politics, in 1912–14, became a matter of indifference after
1919 when the costs seemed to outweigh the benefits.' Any lingering unionist
illusions of Orange-card solidarity faded during the Troubles, and current signs
that the 'Conservative and Unionist' party is morphing into the 'English' party
will come as no surprise. David Trimble may sit with the Tories in the House of
Lords, but he could hardly join *perfide* New Labour, believing as he does that
Tony Blair undermined him by making concessions too easily to Sinn Féin.

Yet on my second count, common interest in the fortunes of 'Britain', there
is paradoxical symmetry between England and Protestant Ulster. They attract
similar elegiac and apocalyptic tropes. Susan McKay's *Northern Protestants: An
Unsettled People*, a tattered Union flag on its jacket, appeared in the same year
(2000) as Andrew Marr's *The Day Britain Died* and Roger Scruton's *England: An
Elegy*. Since they tend to lack a well-maintained 'national' back-up system, cen-
tre and frontier, metropolis and loyal periphery, have most identity to lose
when the ideology that binds a multinational state starts to fray. Thus, if we
have indeed reached the post-Ukanian moment ('Ukania' being Nairn's deri-
sive name for *ancien régime* UK), Scotland and Wales may be better prepared for
change. But is something over, or is it mutating? How prescient was John
Hewitt's allegory 'The Colony' (1953), which identifies Protestant Ulster with
Roman Britain, and speaks in the voice of an unsettled settler?

> ... The danger's there;
> when Caesar's old and lays his sceptre down,
> we'll be a little people, well outnumbered.
>
> Some of us think our leases have run out
> but dig square heels in, keep the roads repaired;
> and one or two loud voices would restore
> the rack, the yellow patch, the curfewed ghetto ...

Most try to ignore the question, going their way,

glad to be living, sure that Caesar's word

is Caesar's bond for legions in our need.

Among us, some, beguiled by their sad music,

make common cause with the natives, in their hearts

hoping to win a truce when the tribes assert

their ancient right and take what once was theirs.

Already from other lands the legions ebb

and men no longer know the Roman peace. …

the rain against the lips, the changing light,

the heavy clay-sucked stride, have altered us;

we would be strangers in the Capitol;

this is our country also, nowhere else;

and we shall not be outcast on the world.

In fact, Ulster Protestants have never really trusted Caesar. After the Anglo-Irish Agreement (to which he was opposed), the historian A.T.Q. Stewart remarked: 'Nothing irritates an Ulsterman more than the assumption that the United Kingdom exists for the comfort and security of England and the English.' Gillian McIntosh's 1999 book on unionist identities, which stops at 1960, has eight index-entries under 'Anglophobia'. McIntosh writes of unionist propaganda:

> [M]any unionists were overtly anglophobic or were, at the very least, hostile towards the British government. Moreover, their sense of history was of a decidedly 'Ulster' variety, and throughout this period they argued for a history which was rooted in Ireland as well as Britain, and specifically in Ulster, focusing on the uniqueness of Ulster and the 'Ulsterman'. In addition to the planter tradition, their connection with

Britain was highlighted in terms of war contributions made by Northern Ireland in the First and Second World Wars.

McIntosh shows that, then as now, Anglophobia had both political causes (economic constraints imposed by Westminster, liberal UK legislation not to unionist taste) and cultural triggers. On the one hand, afraid that 'local' culture might prove too 'Irish', unionists praised the binding role of the BBC: 'The chimes of Big Ben are heard as clearly in Tyrone as ... in the County of Middlesex.' On the other, they complained that English people controlled the BBC in Belfast. For one Stormont MP, Broadcasting House was 'like a foreign country ... We do not want the Oxford accent; we want the Ulster accent'. Today, the full phonetic mosaic of northern Irish Hiberno-English can be heard on BBC Northern Ireland (and further afield), but ideological tension between Ukanianism and Ulsterism persists.

Such attitudes belong to a history of cultural assertion as well as cultural cringe. In *British Identities before Nationalism* (1999) Colin Kidd shows that both pre- and post-Reformation opposition to metropolitan policy could involve a superior if self-serving sense that the 'English in Ireland' were better custodians of fundamental English 'liberties' and values than the English in England: 'Ironically, this heightened sense of an Englishness deprived led in turn to concern for the regnal privileges of the Irish kingdom. It was but a short step from Anglo-Irish unionism to a defiant patriotism.' The Anglo-Irish became capable of seeing themselves as more (rather than less) English or Irish than the 'natives' of either country.

Since Swift, Protestant Ireland has been an ironical vantage point for observing England. Witness the motif of English insensitivity or stupidity. In Maria Edgeworth's novel *Ennui* (1809), Lady Geraldine says of an English visitor:

'... here he comes to hospitable, open-hearted Ireland; eats as well as he can in his own country; drinks better than he can in his own country;

sleeps as well as he can in his own country; accepts all our kindness without a word or a look of thanks, and seems the whole time to think, that "Born for his use, we live but to oblige him". There he is at this instant ... setting down our faults, and conning them by rote.'

In *The Last September* (1929) Elizabeth Bowen comically but pointedly represents Lady Naylor as uniting her own class and the Catholic Irish against the English, when she says of a Catholic neighbour: 'She is a most interesting woman: she thinks a great deal. But then our people do think. Now have you never noticed the English?' Louis MacNeice wrote in 1941: 'Although brought up in the Unionist North, I found myself saturated in the belief that the English are an inferior race. Soft, heavy, gullible, and without any sense of humour ... They were extraordinarily slow in the uptake.' John Hewitt's poem 'A Country Walk in May' (1960), which concerns Ulster people walking in Warwickshire, includes the lines: 'each moment makes our wide divergence plain / from these good-hearted, cocksure, talkative, / more-tolerant-than-any-race-alive, / brave, cosy, but inhospitable folk, who gape at wit and laugh at every joke, / God's Englishmen'. Drew Linden, the protagonist of Glenn Patterson's novel *Fat Lad* (1992), is riled when an English fellow-student at Manchester University sends him a Christmas card in Belfast with an airmail sticker on the envelope: 'Kelly's misconception about the countries' postal relations was no more ludicrous to him than the posturings of the earnest boys who stood every Thursday on the steps of the Union building, with their Harringtons, number one crewcuts, and armfuls of *Troops Out* papers, bellowing in best Home Counties accents – Support the Revolution in Ireland!'

During the last century, 'revolution' has certainly touched Prostestant Ireland more than the Home Counties. Hence the difference between *The Last September* and, say, *Howards End*. When Lady Dorothy Wellesley's English house replaced Coole Park as a symbolic focus for Yeats's value-system, he imposed a factitious grandeur and violence as if requiring intensities that its context could not supply: 'What climbs the stair? / Nothing that common women pon-der on / If you are worth my hope … / The Proud Furies each with her torch on high' ('To Dorothy Wellesley'). In Michael Longley's 'Wounds' (1972) the speaker recalls his English father (who emigrated to Belfast) recalling the Ulster division at the Somme: '"Wilder than Gurkhas" were my father's words / Of admiration and bewilderment'. As violence comes home to Belfast, his father's English shock mediates Longley's perspective as a first-generation de facto Ulster Protestant. Conversely, Peter McDonald, consciously writing as an Ulster Protestant domiciled in England, remembers the Great War in 'Sunday in Great Tew (*8th November 1987*)'. The speaker represents this village as 'a replica of some England, / an idea on show, unchanging, glassy, not quite touchable'. Later he alludes to 'Milton … / po-faced, pig-headed, almost an Ulsterman', and the poem ends with the speaker and his companion 'shut out / from whatever we might be tempted to call our own, / reminded that the dead are close, that here the poppy is an English flower'. These three poems are variously marked by the warfare, *kulturkampf*, intensity and difference of frontier history.

The Miltonic 'Ulsterman' is indeed 'disowned' by England. In *Ulster Loyalism and the British Media* Alan Parkinson finds that, by the early 1970s, 'the British (despite the occasional misdemeanour) took on the mantle of the 'Good', the IRA and Sinn Féin became the 'Bad', and the increasingly less significant Protestants became the 'Ugly' group'. An exception was the 1987 Enniskillen war-memorial bomb, when shared Britishness suddenly counted. In *The English: A Portrait of a People* (1998) Jeremy Paxman observes: 'The paradox is that this great proclamation of belonging [to Britain], that the Ulster "loyal-ists" are in some deep sense the same as the rest of us, merely serves to make them look utterly different.' Paxman may blench at a spectre from the 'deep' English/British past: from seventeenth-century anti-popery, from the Gordon Riots, from the lost hegemonic package of Protestantism, industrialism and empire, from a political unconscious still coping with that loss. His introspective sense of dissolution contemplates a disturbingly extraverted origin. Moreover, his notion that there is something un-British about such extraversion seems predicated on a concept of 'English' reticence which has forgotten the empire and John Bull, let alone the Reformation. Similarly, an English friend, who escorted members of Ian Paisley's Democratic Unionist Party to the Martyrs' Memorial in Oxford, told me that she could not bear to stay there with them, as at a shared tribal totem-pole. After his remarks about Orange parades, Paxman writes: 'the English are no longer quite sure what it is that makes them what they are'. Here Protestant Ulster and England represent poles of over-assertion and understatement, identity-surfeit and identity-deficit, total recall and amnesia.

Yet frontier and metropolitan core are alike in being perceived to carry the primary guilt of a 'colonial' venture, and hence to compromise their own identity-claims. It's not just that Englishness may have been hollowed out by successive expansions, or that Ulster frontiersmen have become 'strangers in the Capitol'. There is also the idea that it takes an experience of oppression to legitimize national or ethnic self-assertion. Hence the English Left's long-standing attraction to nationalism in other people's countries, hence 'Support the Revolution in Ireland', hence Protestants' inexpert attempts to wrest victimhood (Hewitt's 'sad music') from Catholics, as in the self-defeating saga of the Drumcree parade. In autumn 2005 loyalists burned property in their own Belfast neighbourhoods: a professed 'cry of desperation' that seemed more aggressive-passive than passive-aggressive. Right-wing spokesmen for oppressed 'Englishness' also make a poor fist of the poor mouth, as when Roger Scruton complained about 'the forbidding of England' (*Spectator*, 1 April 2000). Ulster Protestants and the English get few sympathy votes.

Of course, English denial or dislike or indifference underlines a crucial asymmetry between core and frontier: asymmetry of power. Hewitt's departing legions, unlike his settlers, have somewhere to go. And, despite Nairn's prophecies, despite devolution, despite the UK's shrunken global position, the

British metropolis is not about to implode like the Hapsburg Empire or Serb-dominated Yugoslavia. 'Declinism' is a more urgent political theme in France. Meanwhile, Ulster unionists are seen and see themselves – the latter perception influences the former – as being in crisis: the institutional and symbolic props of their Britishness gradually kicked away, with London aiding and abetting. British ministers have had to acknowledge the fear, however subjective or propaganda-driven, that Northern Ireland might have become 'a cold house for Protestants'. Yet something has gone cold for the English too. 'Condition of England' books proliferate as Britishness frays across the board. Introducing *Identity of England* (2002), Robert Colls writes: '"England" is always up for debate, of course, but in recent years the debate has become critical.' In *Patriots* (2002) Richard Weight takes for granted the ratchet effect whereby the 'decline of Britishness' signifies a 'late-twentieth-century crisis of English national identity'. The past year has witnessed a few symptoms of Scotophobia, increased preference for the designation 'English' rather than 'British', and a rise in support for an English parliament. Northern Ireland spasmodically enters the picture, but public discussion remains unlikely to take Ian McBride's point: 'While Ulster Unionism is in many ways anomalous, it also reveals, in heightened form, problematic questions about nationality and sovereignty which are rooted in the structure of the United Kingdom itself.' Although Weight promises that Northern Ireland 'is given a central place in this book', Ulster Protestants would find little comfort here since their main role is to underscore the obsolescence of the Britishness they invoke. Yet lessons learned in Northern Ireland are increasingly often cited with reference to Iraq, and perhaps the British question will follow suit.

Arthur Aughey, in contrast, follows the critical-ironical tradition whereby Irish/Ulster Protestants see England as derogating from its own values. In *Nationalism, Devolution and the Challenge to the United Kingdom State* (2001) he ascribes 'the rising note of an English Weltschmerz' to 'identity-sick' intellectuals. Reviewing condition-of-England/Britain writings to date, he favours those that resist apocalyptic panic: 'The English question does need to be addressed – calmly and without hysteria or visionary excess.' He also warns both right-wing and left-wing proponents of a new English sense of nationality against dumping an actually more inclusive and flexible Britishness. He points out, as do others, that non-white communities in England generally prefer 'British', and argues that governance of the devolved Union still requires a strategically blurred line between Englishness and Britishness. To read Aughey's subtext: Ulster unionist self-interest requires English self-suppression. Further, in desiring 'piecemeal change' rather than 'conceptual revolution' in English national consciousness, Aughey defines his own unionism as civic rather than ethnic. To commend the 'rationality' of the UK constitution as a multinational, multicultural framework is implicitly to criticize the ethno-religious identity to which the Democratic Unionists appeal. Yet irrationality and identity-mongering have shaped archipelagic unionism as well as nationalisms. Indeed, belief in the superior rationality of the 'Saxon-Scot' was an ethno-nationalist component of nineteenth-century Britishness.

In *The Making of English National Identity* (2003) Krishan Kumar usefully questions whether a clear line can be drawn between civic and ethnic nationalisms. Citing 'commitment and loyalty to a British monarchy, a British Parliament, a British navy, a British army, a British empire' and 'a common British Protestantism', Kumar observes: 'It does not seem to advance analysis greatly to call all these feelings merely "patriotic loyalty" to "the British state", reserving the term nationalism for some sort of deeper attachment to a "national culture".' He notes how the empire pervaded popular culture (as in Ireland too). Similarly, in *The Nations of Britain* (2006), Christopher Bryant queries the title of Hugh Kearney's influential *The British Isles: A History of Four Nations* (1989): 'Historians do seem to have had inordinate difficulty in addressing the five-nations possibility.'

Nonetheless, most writers on 'Britishness' see it as primarily sustained by constitutional structures and institutional authority. Writing of Britain and

Europe, Andrew Marr observes: 'Britain, being an outward-turned, post-imperial country which is an internal coalition of nations, and now of many smaller communities, has loaded a lot of its public identity onto political traditions and institutions, its separate laws and currency – the very things that Brussels threatens in trying to build an order which will protect entirely different parts of continental life.' Paxman says: 'The English put their faith in institutions, and of these, the British Empire has evaporated, the Church of England has withered away and Parliament is increasingly irrelevant.' As for post-1945 solidarities: Thatcher's market-led assault on the welfare state, the public sphere, trade unionism, the BBC and local government, compounded by New Labour 'modernization', has caused further institutional meltdown. It has removed 'British' from the names and ownership of companies, and rendered Britain (like the Irish Republic) unusually porous to globalization – a second hollowing out. By the law of unintended consequences, Tory and New Labour financialism has eroded Tory and Labour patriotism. David Marquand's *Decline of the Public* (2004) deplores the simultaneous privatization and centralization of the UK state. Civic collectivism has weakened, along with the intermediate institutions and micro-cultures generated by industrial or professional work. Nairn hammers nails into the coffin: 'When the underpinnings of the British state-idea decay, there is surprisingly little left.' And, while not dancing on Britain's grave, contributors to Robert Hazell's *The English Question* (2006) take 'a strongly institutional approach' to (what they agree is) the problem of English self-representation. Hazell, like Marquand, thinks that regionalism's day must come.

New Labour, fearful of Islamism and now led by a Scot, has belatedly put a finger in the collapsing dyke of Britishness. Government ministers Ruth Kelly and Liam Byrne (interesting names) seek to make up the identity-deficit in typically centralist terms. Their proposal for a 'Britain Day' (surely not in Northern Ireland) seems nostalgic for authoritative superstructure, empty as Blair's dome. Noting that official 'Britishness' has always entailed a gap between 'ideality' and particularity, Cairns Craig speculates that 'the "transcendent" cultures of an independent Ireland and an autonomous Scotland are perhaps but the belated repatriation of the cultural capital of a pan-British imperialism'. But, in the case of England, reaction against 'Britain' usually involves a *reversion* to particularity, not a different sublimation of it. This may explain why English regionalism – seen as further superstructure – has been slow to catch on, whereas localism is another matter. In *The Country* (1913) Edward Thomas wrote: 'I wonder how many others feel the same, that we have been robbed ... of the small intelligible England of Elizabeth, and given the word Imperialism instead.' For Roger Scruton, Thomas, together with 'Hardy, Housman ... Elgar, Vaughan Williams and Holst', offers 'the last plaintive invocations of a regional England ... a country of varied agriculture and localised building types, of regional accent and folk song, of local fairs and markets and shows'. Yet Thomas's anti-imperial, localized, ecocentric 'England' was also future-oriented in its vision and critique.

As Britain becomes transcendental, England devolves into detail. Thomas prefaced his wartime anthology *This England* (1915) by calling it 'as full of English character and country as an egg is of meat', and 'never aimed at what a committee from Great Britain and Ireland might call complete'. *England in Particular* (2006), edited by Sue Clifford and Angela King, is a contemporary equivalent. The cover of this alphabetical miscellany represents it as a 'celebration of the commonplace, the local, the vernacular and the distinctive', a championing of 'diversity ... under siege', 'a counterblast against loss and uniformity'. Scruton notes that definitions of Englishness tend to become 'a bundle of sensations'. Commenting on the personal and ephemeral nature of lists like Orwell's 'clatter of clogs in the Lancashire mill towns ... rattle of pintables in the Soho pubs', Scruton asks: 'Is it not obvious that Orwell is describing not a people but a *place* ... For Orwell ... England was not a nation or a creed or a language or a state but a home.' Peter Ackroyd's *Albion* (2002) also stresses place: 'English writers and artists, English composers and folk-

singers, have been haunted by this sense of place, in which the echoic sim-
plicities of past use and past tradition sanctify a certain spot of ground. These
forces are no doubt to be found in other regions and countries of the earth;
but in England the reverence for the past and the affinity with the natural
landscape join together in a mutual embrace'.

Yet Ackroyd's peroration transcends lists of particulars. It suggests that
Romantic England is not dead and gone, and that there is such a thing as
English cultural nationalism even if Britishness has denied or sublimated its
political articulation. Like Scruton, Kumar notices a self-conscious 'moment of
Englishness' – the 'home rule all round' moment, the Edward Thomas
moment – between the late nineteenth century and the Great War. Much still
depends on the matrix wherein modern national identities were configured.
As Aughey stresses, England's 'peculiar sense of nationhood' is not 'the result
of transgressing some law of historical development'. Nor does the possible
end of what Nairn calls 'Anglo-British ambiguity' necessarily expose the
English and Ulster Protestants, co-dependents on the old order, as lacking
identity to fall back on. Even if Britain is breaking up, it need not follow that
they should revert to some theoretically incomplete Herderian project.
Nineteenth-century European nationalism was a *different* matrix for identity-
formation rather than an inevitable stage. Similarly, the Williamite revolution
was not the French Revolution. Nor does Irish nationalism itself owe every-
thing to its nineteenth-century apotheosis (witness its structural Jacobitism),
even if the jury is still out as to whether proto-nationalism existed anywhere
in earlier times. Colin Kidd writes: 'The historic patriotisms of England,
Scotland and Ireland did not function in isolation, but as a system of compet-
ing claims and counter-claims, dominated in the seventeenth century by
tensions within the Stuart multiple monarchy, and in the eighteenth by the
rise of an overarching Britishness.'

Not every ethnicity becomes a nation or wants a state. Nineteenth-century
cultural and political nationalism answered to specific conditions in specific

European countries; and was defined against multi-ethnic frameworks, which yet persisted. Irish cultural nationalists exaggerated differences for the sake of 'de-Anglicisation'. Yet the Herderian spirit touched England and Protestant Ulster too. Eighteenth-century Irish antiquarianism, a complex and cross-sectarian enquiry into origins, had no pre-determined political outcome. If Scottish national identity, to quote Cairns Craig, 'was already enshrined *within* the Act of Union' – he uses the term 'unionist nationalism' – it was no foregone conclusion that Irish national identity would be framed outside it. And, although Paxman measures English exceptionalism by the absence of a national costume or folk-based national songs, nineteenth-century England by no means lacked atavistic literary, musical, linguistic and folkloric forays. While these could be complicit with 'British' ethnic ideology (Saxonism, Gothicism), they more crucially belonged to 'Little England' in its strict localist, anti-imperial meaning. William Morris, who, in David Gervais's words, 'dressed the inhabitants of his Communist Utopia in medieval clothes', and who inspired the Anglo-Irish Yeats and Anglo-Welsh Thomas, was a common archipelagic source.

Because Britishness has often made Englishness invisible or incorrect, there have been relatively few studies of what Gervais, in *Literary Englands* (1993), finds to be a central concern of twentieth-century English writing. Like other critics, Gervais is wary of the pastoral 'nostalgia' to which the pursuit of Englishness is liable: 'Modern England is in danger of becoming a museum of itself.' Ackroyd's *Albion* may exemplify this; Julian Barnes's *England, England* (1998) satirizes it; Peter McDonald's 'Sunday in Great Tew' holds the issue in balance. Yet Patrick Kavanagh, an admirer of Edward Thomas, found the particularism of English country poetry a corrective to both English and Irish nationalism. It's true that the still-influential 'moment of Englishness' was defined in rural rather than urban terms. Yet conservation need not be conservative. Raphael Samuel's *Theatres of Memory* (1994), a left-wing critique of 'heritage-baiting', challenges the indiscriminate amnesia that 'modernizing' ideologies usually entail. The divide over the Hunting with Hounds bill – class war replayed as farce – dramatized obstacles to one-nation Englishness that go beyond the difficulty of reconciling country and city. It illustrated the reflex whereby English intellectuals translate cultural traditions into the (British) terms of right/left politics. The emergent post-industrial compact between Old Labour Wales and Welsh-Wales might be a model for more holistic, not necessarily nationalistic, thinking about English culture.

Contrariwise, a current Ulster unionist attempt at cultural nationalism might be an object-lesson in how not to do it – or in why it ought not to be done. After the Belfast Agreement, *kulturkampf* largely took over from violent confrontation. Some Protestant culture-warriors, who might have pleaded the complexity of their (and their opponents') heritage, unwisely internalized the charge of lacking culture, and went out to get some. The recourse to Scotland, which had answered the idealization of the Irish 'Gael' during the Home Rule period, still centres on the Presbyterian 'Ulster Scot', but with greater stress on 'Ulster Scots' dialect. In fact, 'Ulster Scots' has stretched its linguistic remit to embrace anything Protestant that moves, speaks, sings or dances. One example, in 2004, was the well-attended, lavishly choreographed, historically ludicrous musical *On Eagle's Wing*. Loosely concerned with Ulster Protestant (Scots-Irish) emigration to the US, *On Eagle's Wing* might be dubbed 'kiltsch'. Perhaps Gaelic linguistic nationalism set an unfortunate precedent by basing itself on a language that neither was nor became the main speech of the people. With even greater unreality, the Ulster-Scots Agency has achieved recognition for Ulster Scots as a 'lesser-used' European language, positioning itself on the cross-border language body established under the Agreement. And all this despite scholarly objections to the Agency's separatist concept of 'Ulster Scots' (as distinct from Scots in general), to its neologisms and indefensible orthography, to the dominant role of unionist politicians.

The politicization of the Scots linguistic tradition in Ulster obscures its real cultural interest by imposing an untenable superstructure on oral, textual and contextual specifics. It travesties the historical two-way traffic between Ulster and Scotland. This traffic includes Gaelic-speaking Presbyterians, Scots-speaking Catholics (Seamus Heaney's poetic diction is marked by south Derry Scots), Enlightenment intellectuals, migrant workers, university students (the Ulster Protestant brain-drain to Dundee, Glasgow and Edinburgh), tourists, business people, marching bands, traditional music, Celtic and Rangers supporters, Labourite pro-Union west-of-Scotland Catholics.

But why drop 'Saxon' from 'Scot'? For purposes of unionist nationalism, why not tease out the English strands in Ulster's historical weave? Presbyterians (including breakaway sects like Paisley's) outnumber Anglicans, but not hugely. Both the English language and Anglicanism, however, confuse many issues by extending to London and Dublin, by implicating the poetry of George Herbert and Yeats as well as Derek Mahon. On top of the Anglophobia and Anglican-phobia already packed into Presbyterian baggage from Scotland, other factors may disqualify England from symbolically functioning as the ethnic bedrock. To sections of Protestant Ulster, English horizons are suspect historically as the Dublin-centred Anglo-Irish hegemony which discriminated against nonconformists, and suspect socially as that upper echelon of the Protestant bourgeoisie which allegedly opts out of politics, imagines itself as living in the Home Counties, wants its children to go to Oxbridge rather than Dundee, and is snobbish about 'dialect'. Unionism itself used to be more like this.

Despite pan-Protestant unity in the wake of Catholic emancipation, old fissures remain. Writing on the siege of Derry, John Kerrigan captures still-recognizable differences: 'One might … contrast the geopolitical vision of a sermon preached to the garrison by the Church of Ireland Walker, who, despite his Scottish origins, emphasised the English stem of Ulster Protestantism, going back to the Henrician reformation, with that of a sermon by the Presbyterian Seth Whittle, in which Derry is an isolated Jerusalem that puts no trust in princes.' (Kerrigan shows that Presbyterian/Anglican tensions in Derry and Down fed back into English politics too.) Thus the DUP's rise might be seen as both de-Anglicizing and de-Anglicanizing Ulster unionism. Ballymena is less English than north Down, and Paisleyism represents a genuine if 'altered' (Hewitt) Scottish presence in Ulster. Despite their different politics, Paisley and Alex Salmond collaborating as devolved First Ministers sets off strange resonances. Yet, of course, masses of elite and popular culture derive from England, and Ulster Protestant allegiance has not been only to Tory Britain. Hewitt's sense of his intellectual heritage stresses English radicalism, itself influenced by the Ulster-Scottish Enlightenment. He wrote in 1972: 'My mother tongue is English, instrument and tool of my thought and expression: John Ball, the Diggers, the Levellers, the Chartists, Paine, Morris … the British democratic tradition.'

It may be difficult to pin down Ulster Protestant and English cultural identity (if we want to pin down identity at all), partly because England and the north of Ireland are areas where the history of these islands – invasions, migrations, reformations – has left unusually compacted traces. Since both, up to a point, are archipelagic microcosms, almost too much identity is on offer. For Peter Conrad, 'the history of the English imagination is the history of adaptation and assimilation, Englishness is the principle of diversity itself'. 'Diversity' was being debated in Northern Ireland before becoming an issue in Britain, and 'the principle of diversity' defines contemporary northern Irish poetry as much as it does English literary history. The poetry's linguistic self-consciousness and intertextual reach show that it has been able to absorb, recombine and reinvent many strands that have historically constituted the English lyric. While such complexity may be hard to read, simplified identity-claims are no solution. Although Paxman believes that those 'countries which do best in the world … have a coherent sense of their own culture', coherence is not an axiomatic virtue. Most cultural nationalisms ignore most culture. They plaster over huge cracks that eventually cause subsidence. Monocular Ulster-Scottishness, like archaic Britishness, paints Ulster Protestants into a corner.

Complex versions of Englishness, usually conceived by writers in times of war, usually taking their cue from English literature, stress metamorphosis rather than elegy – or snatch metamorphosis from elegy. Virginia Woolf's condition-of-England novel *Between the Acts* (1941) centres on a village pageant that enacts the course of English history as war looms. The spectators expect the pageant to express traditional British patriotism, but are frustrated by the subversive designs of its director (a mask for Woolf herself) who exploits the gap between the local actors and the still-imperial state. When the pageant reaches 'Present time. Ourselves', the cast holds up mirrors that both particularize and destabilize the audience's identity: 'the looking glasses darted, flashed, exposed'. A refrain of both pageant and novel is 'Unity – Dispersity': 'The gramophone gurgled *Unity – Dispersity*. It gurgled *Un … dis*. And ceased.'

'Un … dis' echoes beyond 1939. Robert Colls concludes that, while the institutional forms of Englishness/Britishness have lost much of their consensual validity and appeal, historical 'memory' remains a crucial point of reference. And: 'In searching for a new *modus vivendi*, the nation's propensity for seeing itself as diverse should not be allowed to outstrip its propensity for seeing itself as unified.' The challenge for Ulster Protestants is how to get beyond the binary of Ulsterism and Ukanianism, while also accommodating (or reshaping) 'Irishness'. Poetry may offer a parable for these dilemmas. It's certainly an anomaly, perhaps a 'forbidding of England', that no anthologies of modern or contemporary *English* poetry exist. Where anthologies are not Irish, Scottish, Welsh or English-regional, they are now scrupulously 'British and Irish'. An 'English' anthology should not be problematic, especially now that 'Englishness' is being opened up in literary studies. Thus Randall Stevenson's *The Last of England?* (2004), final volume of the *Oxford English Literary History*, 'concentrates more firmly than its predecessors on writing in England [1960–2000], separately from the traditions of neighbouring nations, or other anglophone ones abroad'. Stevenson also notices that a 'new interest in separateness, and in separate traditions, began to appear in literature itself in the 1990s'. Yet he may simply be catching up with something always there. And his apparent doubt as to whether he is writing an elegy or saluting a metamorphosis suggests that he is attempting an impossible contraction. Since modern Irish and Scottish literary studies are just emerging from unduly separatist paradigms, it would be a pity if 'English studies' were to atone for Britishness and hegemonic 'Eng Lit' by reinventing the nationalist literary-critical wheel. In any case, national anthologies need their 'British and Irish' complement as well as further inter-national vistas. 'Diversity', as poetic traditions, operates between as well as within nations. Northern Irish poetry poses particularly awkward questions for national literary histories.

Histories of the Anglo-Scottish Union, the rise of Irish-Scottish studies, books about Englishness that leak in every direction: all this contributes to an archipelagic paradigm. Besides the timely new edition of *The British Isles: A History of Four Nations*, Hugh Kearney has just published *Ireland: Contested Ideas of Nationalism and History*. In an introductory reprise of his intellectual journey, Kearney touches different bases: Anglocentric imperial history and its deconstruction; Scottish unionist history and its fears; Irish nationalist and 'revisionist' history; 'Atlantic' or 'New British' history. Kearney is exemplary in having so finely tracked the intricacies of affiliation, difference and contestation that make up the archipelagic cat's cradle. It is, of course, politically urgent for Northern Irish people to accept that strands continue across both the Irish border and the Irish Sea. The more closely you scan the region (as the poetry), the more complex its patchwork of particulars, the more it resists reductive cultural politics. The devil, and the parallel with England, is in the detail.

Andrew Marr wrote in 2000: 'We either embark on an ambitious and risky plan of further democratic reform – an English Parliament, federal Britain, a written constitution – or we will end up, one day, in a chilly churchyard of the mind, throwing handfuls of clay on the Union Flag.' This seems to place England and Protestant Ulster at the same bleak crossroads. An alternative scenario (the books cited here mostly end with alternative scenarios) is that the Belfast Agreement, which several authors invoke, portends further constructive shifts in a European and global context that is transforming the terms of national sovereignty. But Northern Ireland's present leadership, compared by David Trimble to the Hitler-Stalin pact, is as yet an oxymoron rather than an elision or intercultural beacon. And, especially in loyalist-controlled districts, racism or hostility to immigrants may be the new sectarianism. Even so, the angel is in the devolutionary detail too. On the ground, in many economic and cultural endeavours, a dynamic between common 'northern' points of reference and wider orbits now has more scope to shake fixed positions.

As 'Northern Ireland' must over-spill borders and be over-spilt (new road and air routes are the tangible sign of this), so 'England' must absorb new waves of diversity that are changing its particulars once again. According to Robert Colls (*Prospect*, July 2007), demographers expect 'national ancestry' to be 'radically and permanently altered by high levels of immigration'. For Krishan Kumar it would be tragic if the English reacted by 'coming to see themselves within the terms of a narrow English nationalism' rather than by epitomizing an 'open' and 'diverse' society. For Christopher Bryant, a 'cosmopolitan England could accumulate more differences' than can be accommodated if it fails to mediate the English/British past. Similarly, in his *Prospect* article as in *Identity of England*, Colls stresses 'memory'. He argues that national identity is based 'on a common view of historical relationships' but also that circumstances may rearrange and complicate the view – a process well underway with respect to Northern Ireland – and thus 'prepare us for other cultures in a century that is going to be mesmerised by [them]'. Given what 'Present time. Ourselves' shows in the mirror, both metropolis and frontier could find heterogeneity an asset rather than a handicap. Today there are strangers in all the Capitols.

BIBLIOGRAPHY
Peter Ackroyd, *Albion: The Origins of the English Imagination* (London: Chatto & Windus, 2002); Arthur Aughey, *Nationalism, Devolution and the Challenge to the United Kingdom State* (London: Pluto, 2001); Christopher G.A. Bryant, *The Nations of Britain* (Oxford: Oxford

University Press, 2006); Sue Clifford & Angela King, *England in Particular* (London: Hodder & Stoughton, 2006); Robert Colls, *Identity of England* (Oxford: Oxford University Press, 2002); Cairns Craig, 'Constituting Scotland', *Irish Review* 28 (Winter 2000), 'National literature and cultural capital in Ireland and Scotland' in (eds) Liam McIlvanney & Ray Ryan, *Ireland and Scotland: Culture and Society 1700–2000* (Dublin: Four Courts, 2005); Ruth Dudley Edwards, *The Faithful Tribe: An Intimate Portrait of the Loyal Institutions* (London: HarperCollins, 1999); David Gervais, *Literary Englands: Versions of 'Englishness' in Modern Writing* (Cambridge: Cambridge University Press, 1993); Robert Hazell (ed.), *The English Question* (Manchester: Manchester University Press, 2006); John Hewitt, *Ancestral Voices: The Selected Prose of John Hewitt*, (ed.) Tom Clyde (Belfast: Blackstaff, 1987); Hugh Kearney, *The British Isles: A History of Four Nations* (Cambridge: Cambridge University Press, 1989; new edn, 2006), *Ireland: Contested Ideas of Nationhood and History* (Cork: Cork University Press, 2007); John Kerrigan, 'Ulster and the New British Histories: Milton to Mitchelbourne', in (eds) Eamonn Hughes, Edna Longley & Des O'Rawe, *Ireland (Ulster) Scotland: Concepts, Contexts, Comparisons* (Belfast: Clo Ollscoil na Banriona, 2003); Colin Kidd, *British Identities before Nationalism: Ethnicity and Nationhood in the Atlantic World 1600–1800* (Cambridge: Cambridge University Press, 1999); Krishan Kumar, *The Making of English National Identity* (Cambridge: Cambridge University Press, 2003); Ian McBride, 'Ulster and the British Problem', in (eds) Richard English & Graham Walker, *Unionism in Modern Ireland* (Dublin: Gill and Macmillan, 1996); Peter McDonald, *Biting the Wax* (Newcastle upon Tyne: Bloodaxe, 1989); Gillian McIntosh, *The Force of Culture: Unionist Identities in Twentieth-Century Ireland* (Cork: Cork University Press, 1999); Susan McKay, *Northern Protestants: An Unsettled People* (Belfast: Blackstaff, 2000); Louis MacNeice, *The Poetry of W.B. Yeats* (London: Faber, 1967); Andrew Marr, *The Day Britain Died* (London: Profile, 2000); Alan F. Parkinson, *Ulster Loyalism and the British Media* (Dublin: Four Courts, 1998); Tom Nairn, *After Britain* (London: Granta, 2000); Jeremy Paxman, *A Portrait of the English People* (London: Penguin, 1998); Roger Scruton, *England: An Elegy* (London: Chatto & Windus, 2000); Randall Stevenson, *The Last of England?* (Oxford: Oxford University Press, 2004); Edward Thomas, *The Country* (London: B.T. Batsford, 1913); John Turner, 'Letting go: The Conservative Party and the end of the Union with Ireland', in (eds) Alexander Grant & Keith J. Stringer, *Uniting the Kingdom?* (London: Routledge, 1995); Richard Weight, *Patriots: National Identity in Britain 1940–2000* (London: Macmillan, 2002); Virginia Woolf, *Between the Acts* (London: Penguin, 2000).

Our own George Clooney

MOLLY McCLOSKEY

1

In his book *Happiness*, the Buddhist monk Matthieu Ricard tells the story of a King of Persia who instructed his loyal scribe to produce a history of mankind so that he could draw the necessary lessons and see the best way to proceed. After consulting with historians, scholars and sages, the scribe presented the king with a history in thirty-six volumes. Naturally, the king hadn't time to read this and told the scribe to condense it, which he did – to ten volumes. By then, war was raging and the king had even less time for reading. He asked the scribe to cut the history to a single volume; the scribe complied. Even this was too much, however, and the king requested tenfold fewer pages and promised to read them in an evening. But by the time the scribe returned, the king was on his deathbed. With his final breath, the king asked, *Well, what of the history of men?* In the ultimate abridgement, his loyal scribe replied, *They suffer.*

For a year it was my job to report on Somalia for the UN's Office for the Coordination of Humanitarian Affairs. With my colleagues in the information department I produced 'public situation reports' (or 'sitreps'), monthly humanitarian analyses, press releases, internal reports to the UN's Emergency Relief Coordinator, talking points for various meetings and PowerPoint pre-sentations. All of this information-gathering and dissemination was done so that we – our office and the UN agencies and NGOs with which we worked – could draw the necessary lessons and see the best way to proceed. Mostly, the hundreds of thousands of words I produced on the plight of Somalis boiled down to: *They suffer.*

Because the office is based in Nairobi, and because language has a way of detaching itself from its own referents, Somali misery often seemed unreal. We sometimes used the phrase 'unnecessary suffering', usually when issuing a press release begging people to stop killing each other, suggesting that there was a kind of suffering, or a level, that was necessary and that we were all in agreement on what that was. In the early months of my job, I heard of 58,000 children suffering from malnutrition. I heard the figure so many times that I came to imagine them as a single entity – a band of stick figures, 58,000 strong, shuffling across the arid wastelands. The language of malnutrition is unsettling, with its clinical references to MUAC (mid-upper-arm circumference), its life-saving formula titled like a tax form (the therapeutic milk F75), and the oft-coupled GAM and SAM, which sound like a comic duo but stand instead for the potentially lethal states of Global and Severe Acute Malnutrition.

Some of what I wrote was based on reports we received from our Somali colleagues in the field. They also sent us photos – of locusts and emaciated cattle and starving children, of withered crops and child soldiers and people missing limbs. One day, out of an impulse I could only guess at, a colleague sent us eleven pictures of the sunset over Gedo.

Of the 265 UN international staff currently involved with operations in Somalia, only 86 are based in the country itself. None of these (save two security staff) are in Mogadishu, where the UN has not had a permanent international humanitarian presence since 1995. (There are currently 70 Somalis working for UN agencies in Mogadishu.) The rest of the UN international staff dealing with Somalia – including the Humanitarian Coordinator and all Heads of Agencies – are based in Nairobi; all high-level decision-making takes place in Nairobi. Between two-day or two-week trips to Somalia, internationals enjoy relatively luxurious lives, and there is no doubt that being in Nairobi left us somewhat out of touch. As one of my Somali colleagues used to remind me, there is Nairobi-Somalia and Somalia-Somalia. The reason the mission is run from outside the country is, of course, that Somalia is (and has for some time been) unstable and unsafe. But there is a feeling in Somalia, among the general population and the authorities, that the money spent keeping us in Nairobi would be better spent on the humanitarian needs of Somalis.

2

Flying in to Wajid on my first visit to Somalia, we passed over brown arid fields that looked capable of producing nothing and yet were divided into small careful squares, as though by a stick, the way a volleyball court might be marked out on a flat stretch of beach. Located in the South/Central zone, Wajid, with its tiny airfield, was jokingly referred to as a 'hub'. (I was in transit, on my way to Hargeisa in Somaliland, the north-western region that had claimed independence from Somalia in 1994.) UN and NGO workers slouched on the concrete benches, waiting to fly further into Somalia or back to Nairobi, and a Somali man sold souvenirs – old Italian coins and milk gourds and jewellery. Beyond the airstrip's boundaries, plastic bags (bleached by the sun to the palest pastels) bloomed on thorny shrubs.

This was August 2006 and South/Central Somalia – and particularly Mogadishu – was enjoying a season of relative peace. Since 1991, when regional insurgent groups had overthrown the dictator Siad Barre and then turned on each other, warlords – each with his own militia – had run Mogadishu and other parts of South/Central. But between June and August, fighters of the Islamic Courts Union had defeated the US-backed group of warlords known as the Alliance for the Restoration of Peace and Counter-Terrorism, and had taken control of the capital and much of the surrounding region. In the space of a few weeks the ICU had done what two internationally backed governments, two UN missions and the American military had failed to do: tame Mogadishu.

Was this good news? In a way, yes. The people of Mogadishu were reported to be happy. Not necessarily because they were keen on Shari'a law (Somalia's brand of Sufi Islam is essentially moderate, and the Somali population in general has been regarded as far too individualistic to embrace an extremist agenda) but because anything was better than the warlords. The citizens shown celebrating on CNN weren't choosing between liberal democracy and the veil. They were choosing between chaos and predictability. They wanted, like people everywhere, to be able to go from one end of town to the other without being taxed, robbed, shot at, raped or murdered. And the ICU, for the most part, was enabling this. The ubiquitous checkpoints and roadblocks had been dismantled, and freedom of movement had greatly increased. A clean-up campaign was underway around the city.

The mood in our office and among the humanitarian organizations we worked with was one of guarded optimism – though the levels of guardedness and optimism varied considerably. There was little doubt that the rise of the ICU represented a sea change in Somalia; it just wasn't clear what direction the change would take. In August, the ICU established an office to 'coordinate humanitarian agencies', expressing in a communiqué both their 'respect' for such agencies for having provided assistance to Somalis during fifteen years of lawlessness and their condolences to the families and friends of those who had lost their lives in the effort. The ICU document pledged to respect international conventions relating to aid workers and to ensure the security of expatriate and local humanitarian staff. However, it quickly became apparent that a schism was brewing in the ICU, with the extremists seemingly in the ascendant. In addition, a radical jihadist wing – the Shabaab (meaning 'youth') – had formed, committed to the establishment of an Islamic state through armed revolution and reportedly rejecting any dealings with international aid organizations.

There was disagreement between New York and Nairobi as to whether the UN's Somalia operation should have direct dealings with the head of the radical element in the ICU, Sheikh Hassan Dahir Aweys. The UN's humanitarian arm in Nairobi was arguing that it should have the right to speak to anyone who could help it to gain access to people in need of assistance, while policy people in New York – mindful of the awkward fact that three ICU leaders were on a UN 'blacklist' of people suspected of ties to Al-Qaeda – resisted the idea. Meanwhile, the UN's Humanitarian Coordinator for Somalia, along with various heads of UN agencies, had begun travelling to Mogadishu to meet with non-blacklisted members of the ICU about humanitarian access and assistance. The Humanitarian Coordinator never met directly with Aweys. Still, when he returned from meetings with the Islamists, there was a whiff of sulfur about him.

3

Our office was heavily involved in 'advocacy'. More effective advocacy with all 'stakeholders' could help us to increase humanitarian access and the level of assistance delivered. We hired a consultant for six months to develop an 'advocacy strategy', and in September 2006 we had an 'advocacy workshop' in Nairobi to discuss and refine strategies. UN agencies and international and Somali NGOs were present. Much of the time was spent delineating how Somalis viewed the international community and how, through better advocacy, we could correct the misperceptions (e.g., that we were actually all spies working for the CIA) and address the more legitimate criticisms (e.g., that our numerous assessments were too seldom followed by assistance).

The day involved much self-flagellation among the non-Somalis. We didn't listen to Somalis. We didn't 'share ownership' with them. We failed to display enough cultural sensitivity. We were arrogant and ignorant and basically useless. The self-criticism seemed to arise from an insistence on our taking sole responsibility for everything that was wrong with Somalia. What we didn't discuss that day – though what everyone there knew about – were things like the occasional attacks by Somalis on UN World Food Programme convoys; the fact that local authorities manipulated and misused aid by insisting it be distributed

on the basis of clan; that aid agencies had for the past several years been pay-
ing exorbitant fees at checkpoints in order to move aid across the country;
that Somalis on the UN payroll in programmes to eradicate female genital
mutilation continued to have their daughters mutilated; that often there was
no work done after midday because that was when the khat-chewing began
and that it was virtually impossible to rebuild a country on four hours' work
a day.

It was generally agreed at the workshop that the world suffered from
Somalia fatigue. We were all sadly aware that Somalia and its cycle of misery
were not 'sexy'. So one of the issues of the day was: how could we raise the
profile of Somalia and reawaken the world to the scale of suffering that has
become routine for its people? As Darfur was then enjoying the attentions of
Hollywood, a woman from UNICEF said, in what seemed one of the more can-
did suggestions of the day, 'We need our own George Clooney.'

4

Gerald Hanley was born in Liverpool of Irish parents, worked for the BBC and,
as an officer in the British army, was stationed in Somalia during the Second
World War. He wrote *Warriors*, one of the most beloved and respected books
on Somalia, while living in Kenya in the mid 1960s and after having made a
brief return to Mogadishu, docking there for a day and wandering the streets,
beset both by nostalgia and by 'memories of brutal things'. To say that *Warriors*
is 'about' Somalia is certainly true, because the book captures the essence of
the place to such a degree that one easily recognizes it sixty years later. But it
would only partially do justice to a book that begins:

*True solitude is when the most restless part of a human being, his longing to forget where
he is, born on earth in order to die, comes to rest and listens in a kind of agreed peace. In*

solitude, once the taste has settled, a man can think upon death with as much pleasure as upon life, and it is in solitude that one can best understand that there is no solution, except to try and do as little harm as possible while we are here, that there is no losing and no winning, no real end to greed or lust, because the human appetite for novelty can only be fully satisfied by death.

Thousands of days and nights spent in wilderness taught me that a person can never truly know another, or be known by another, and the pleasure of life is in the trying. A man can never convey fully what it is that so strangely disturbs him, the uneasy unrest in him that nothing material can properly satisfy.

Moving to the particulars of Somalia, Hanley continues:

One had years of wilderness in which to brood on the reasons why men kill each other, in wilderness in which killing a man was only an act of pleasure, though disguised as a tribal duty. One had years to discover that one's longing for mail, newspapers, radio, could slowly diminish. After Somalia nowhere would ever be lonely, or isolated, again. The silence of wilderness eventually seeps in and makes an area which will always long for that kind of silence again.

One was mad, all right, after a year of it. One sees that now, looking back.

Madness, and the attempted avoidance of it, is a theme in *Warriors*. As dangerous as it was to be stationed among clans with enduring blood feuds, the threats to one's sanity were equally severe, and Hanley returns repeatedly to the task of learning how to live with one's own mind in the 'vast insane asylum' that was Somalia. He knew seven comrades who committed suicide there and fifteen cases of madness. He himself was fourteen months in Somalia – with its burning winds and incandescent light – before he got his first leave.

His descriptions of everyday life at his various posts in Somalia are often as lyrical as the passages on loneliness, isolation and madness. He admired the

Somalis for their wit, pride, vanity and restlessness, but felt contempt for their easy brutality and refused to romanticize them. ('There is nothing fine or noble about savagery and illiteracy and superstition, no matter how splendid looking the warriors and the women.') Ever mindful of the slaughter taking place in Europe at the time, Hanley never exalted the European either, who was not so 'innocently honest' about his savagery.

Somalia, what I saw of it in five visits to various parts of the country, wasn't shocking. It was exactly like the six o'clock news and the front page of your newspaper: skinny guys in rags with AK-47s hanging from shoulder straps or held loosely in their hands as though they'd forgotten they were there and were for the purpose of killing. Because a Somali in rags with an AK-47 has become such an iconic media image, these young men seemed not quite real, or simply to be playing the part of themselves in a drama that has had far too long a run.

There were pleasant surprises, though. How quiet the world still is without piped music and the white-noise overflow from iPods. The coloured drawings on the outer walls of shops, skilful and ironic, like illustrations in a graphic novel. (These drawings represented what went on inside, though there was a certain amount of wishful thinking at work: the outer walls of a café showed T-bone steaks and thick juicy hamburgers with all the trimmings; gleaming appliances adorned the walls of an electrics store; on the outside of a pharmacy a great array of medicines were painted, as well as a syringe dripping blood.) There was black humour and a love of the absurd. There were the children – deferential, unaggressive, capable of wonder: like how we imagine Western children used to be.

And there were individuals who – in spite of floods, droughts, locusts, senseless killings, proxy wars, corruption, cholera and countless other soul-destroying realities – still managed to try; people who got up every morning and did work that nobody outside of their village (or the donor supporting their endeavours) would ever hear about. There were men who were genuine feminists, men who had somehow sprouted, like desert flowers, in the midst of all that backwardness. There was the young man in Wajid who pointed to the palm of his hand to illustrate what his wife's sewn-shut vagina had been like before they were married; who had travelled secretly with her to Baidoa before the wedding to find a doctor who could, as painlessly and safely as possible, reverse the damage; who described her five days of often unconscious labour which ended in a stillbirth, and who didn't need to be coached by international gender experts to know that it was all an abomination.

5

In September 2006, shortly after the advocacy workshop, our young Italian desk officer flew over from New York and the two of us travelled together to Wajid. Sophia was on a 'familiarization mission' and I was writing about a Therapeutic Feeding Centre run by Action Contre la Faim for a montly publication issued by our office. I was curious about Wajid – strange stories had been filtering back to Nairobi about the UN compound there, which housed several internationals, mostly from the World Food Programme and World Health Organization. It was said living conditions were appalling, visitors were unwelcome and heavy drinking long into the night was the norm. I had visions of Kurtz in *Heart of Darkness*, people gone totally round the bend.

One was mad, all right, after a year of it …

As it was, the people in the compound just seemed ill-tempered, tired and frustrated. They knew that all of Nairobi had heard about them, and there was a certain defensiveness in the air; Sophia and I felt a little like colonial officers sent to check on the outposts.

For three days we sat at the long wooden table in the hut of the compound, meeting people from UN agencies, NGOs and the District Commissioner of

Wajid, and we visited various projects in and around the area. At the Therapeutic Feeding Centre, we were led into a wattle hut where a small shapeless form was sleeping under the blanket, isolated, because he probably had tuberculosis. This was Kafey. He was two years old and had arrived half an hour before. His father, Noor, who was gazing at Kafey just like we were, said it had taken him five days to carry his son to the centre. Kafey had already received his first meal of F75. He was one of the more fortunate of the 58,000 (a two-month-old brother had died of malnutrition during the previous year's drought). As we left the hut, I asked the translator what Noor had said at the end, just before we'd said goodbye. What Noor had said was that it was all his wife's fault that his children suffered from malnutrition. She wasn't being a proper mother.

We left the Centre, riding past the red-earth anthills that rose as high as the roof of our Land Cruiser. Primordial and alive, the anthills unnerved me in a way the guns did not. We were going back into town, to sit in on a sex education class for girls at the World Vision Wajid FGM Resources Centre, a programme supported by the Finnish government. The class, run by the African Medical and Research Foundation and World Vision, had about twenty-five girls, and the local sheikh was sitting in. The Somali teachers – one man and one woman – showed a video called 'Let Us Talk', made by people in the Somali diaspora in Denmark advocating against female genital mutilation. Habiba, the woman teacher, drew detailed sex organs on a flip chart.

The film opened with a re-enactment of a circumcision, complete with bloodied sewing needle. The scene was followed by the now-circumcised teenage girl saying to her father, 'Why don't you just cut us in pieces?', which elicited knowing, ironic chuckles from the girls in the class.

There are two kinds of so-called female circumcision. The milder form, known as Female Genital Cutting (FGC), or *Sunna*, involves cutting away the tip of the clitoris, while Female Genital Mutilation (FGM) – also called

Pharaonic circumcision or infibulation – involves total removal of the clitoris and labia minora and the stitching together of the labia majora, leaving a small opening which allows urine and menstrual discharge to pass but which prevents sexual intercourse. The operation is mostly carried out by traditional midwives or circumcisers using unsterilized instruments such as knives, razors or even broken glass, and without anaesthesia.

Complications of FGM include genital malformation and damage to the reproductive organs, chronic pelvic complications, difficulty urinating and recurrent urinary tract infection. Blood accumulates at menstruation and can cause repeated infections, blood poisoning and sterility. When girls marry, they must be re-cut to enable intercourse, and childbirth is prone to numerous complications, not least the foetus having his or her head crushed in the damaged birth canal. Before childbirth, mothers must often be cut open again – through thickened scar tissue – to allow the baby to emerge. Fistula, which is usually caused by several days of obstructed labour, can occur as a direct consequence of FGM (the soft tissues of the pelvis are pressed between the descending baby's head and the mother's pelvic bone; the lack of blood flow causes tissue to die, creating a hole between the mother's vagina and bladder and resulting in chronic urinary incontinence). FGM increases a woman's vulnerability to contracting HIV. The growth of scar tissue around the sexual organs leaves little possibility for sexual pleasure. Finally, there is the loss of libido, which would seem a blessing given all of the above, were it not for the fact that (according to UNICEF) two thirds of Somali women believe their husbands are justified in beating them if they refuse sex.

The latest and most comprehensive survey on women and children released by UNICEF puts the prevalence of FGM/FGC in Somalia at 98 per cent, with the prevalence of the extreme form of mutilation at 77 per cent. Most girls are circumcised between the ages of five and nine. FGM/FGC is what the UN refers to as a 'harmful cultural practice', and it is cultural rather than strictly religious. Not all Muslim societies practise it, and many non-Muslim societies do. However, religious leaders have been slow to speak publicly against it, and many Somalis believe that FGM is a religious obligation.

That afternoon, we spent more time with Habiba, who runs a safe house for women who suffer from fistula and are trying to reach Ethiopia for reconstructive surgery. Just then, she had four women living with her, wearing Pampers and waiting to go to Addis.

On our last day, Sophia and I set out with two colleagues who were based in Wajid – a Liberian and a Somali – to drive to Hudur, a couple of hours northeast. As UN security required non-Somali staff travelling by road in that area to be escorted by at least one armed guard – who had to ride in a separate vehicle – we were a convoy of two, our local security having been approved by Wajid's District Commissioner. We had travelled only a few minutes on the dirt road when our way was blocked by a burnt-orange pick-up truck parked across the road. Both Land Cruisers stopped, and our driver got out, as did the armed guard from the escort vehicle. The driver of the orange pick-up remained in his car. Shouting ensued, which wasn't necessarily cause for alarm as Somalis, like Italians, shout for no reason at all. It became clear that the dispute was about the hiring of the escort vehicle – a common cause of tension, and sometimes violence, in Somalia, where employment is so scarce.

Sophia and I waited nervously in the back of the Land Cruiser (was the driver of the pick-up armed? wasn't the shouting becoming more heated? didn't our Liberian colleague appear worried?) until I noticed our security guy, his AK-47 hanging in that half-forgotten way, putting a finger to the side of his nose and blowing loudly into the dirt. He was devoting much attention to this activity, which I took as a good sign. How serious could things be if our security guard was more worried about blowing his nose than about the unfolding row? Finally, after much shouting, gesticulating, nose-blowing, walking away and coming back, it was agreed that in order to avoid escalation of the dispute we would use the orange pick-up and send back the car we'd started with. It seemed like a bad idea to me, given that the driver of the pick-up was agitated and aggressive, but our Somali colleague had already gotten into the back. Sophia and I hesitated. Nothing moved. Heated discussion flared once more. Then, mysteriously, our Somali colleague got out of the pick-up again, and the driver turned back towards Wajid. Having won the argument, the driver had announced that, actually, he hadn't enough fuel to drive us to Hudur.

6

Sister Leonella Sgorbati was murdered in Mogadishu on 17 September 2006, in broad daylight, along with her escort. I heard about it at 6 a.m. the following morning when I was on the way to the Nairobi airport to fly to Somaliland. The sixty-five-year-old nun, who spoke fluent Somali and had worked in Africa for nearly forty years, was shot three times in the back outside a women and children's hospital. The ICU condemned the killing and reportedly arrested three men in connection with it, but stated that they could not guarantee the security of international humanitarian staff. The murder had come in the wake of the Pope's recent controversial comments about Islam and it was rumoured to be in retaliation.

The following day, there was an attempt on the life of the President of Somalia's official but ineffectual Transitional Federal Government, as he left the Parliament building in Baidoa. (The TFG, established in 2004 through an agreement between regional militias and political leaders, and backed by the Western powers, had never managed to sit in Mogadishu.) The two explosions, which caused eleven deaths, were thought to have involved a suicide bomber, marking the first time that the tactic had been employed in Somalia. I was in Somaliland to visit a project run by the UN High Commission for Refugees and a Somali NGO that offered counselling to victims of sexual violence in settlements for internally displaced people. When news of the assassination reached our office in Hargeisa, my Somali colleague said, 'Come in and watch the bomb on the internet!'

Somalis in the office were chuckling. 'Now we are like Iraq!' they said.

In Puntland, the semi-autonomous zone in the north-east of Somalia, a 'day of anger' was planned for that week, to protest against the Pope's comments. Also, there had been a death threat against our head of security by a group calling itself the Somalia Islamic Defence Force (SIDF). The letter promised to kill our security chief if he did not stay out of Somalia and pull all other security staff out. The SIDF did not wish to harm other UN agencies, which it noted had clear mandates and activities, but they *just knew* that because our security department did not itself deliver humanitarian assistance, it could only be involved in one thing: collecting information for 'the Jewish and Americans'. The evidence for this was that security staff members used Thuraya satellite phones and VHF radios (in fact every UN staff member in Somalia is required to carry such equipment). Meanwhile, we had heard that the Shabaab – the radical youth wing of the ICU, which had been accused of involvement in the murder of Sister Leonella – had declared the UN legitimate targets. On 19 September, it was announced that all UN international staff would be temporarily relocated to Nairobi from South/Central and Puntland and all missions to Mogadishu suspended until further notice.

7

In October, the rains came. The previous spring's rains had not materialized and Somalia had experienced its worst drought in over a decade. Now, forecasts for some regions called for the worst flooding in fifty years.

By mid November virtually all riverine villages in some districts were either flooded or surrounded by floodwater. Several were inaccessible even by boat. Malaria and diarrhoea were on the rise. Crocodiles and snakes were terrorizing the population (nine people had already been eaten by crocodiles). People were climbing trees to escape, eating leaves to survive.

Around UN offices in Nairobi, there was a certain adrenaline rush. For a humanitarian operation hampered in its capacity to deliver sustained assistance, it seemed that, finally, we could do something. Our own office received temporary additional staff from an emergency roster in Geneva; some of them stayed in Nairobi writing a fundraising appeal, while others went to Somalia to help with logistics. (The September relocation of international staff to Nairobi had been short-lived.) A special World Food Programme helicopter operation was launched. Moving aid overland had become difficult or impossible; several WFP trucks were stranded along flooded roads. We had 8 a.m. inter-agency meetings on Saturdays and Sundays.

By early December over 400,000 people were estimated to have been displaced by floods; it was expected that if the flooding continued through the month, the number displaced could reach 900,000. Though it lacked technical expertise, the ICU was eager to act. It established an Emergency Relief and Flood Committee and promised humanitarian agencies 'full cooperation', appealing publicly in a communiqué for urgent assistance.

Meanwhile, there were rumours of war.

Ethiopian troops had been in Somalia for several months, protecting the Transitional Federal Government's position in Baidoa, trying to quell an Islamist expansion that could destabilize Ethiopia's own internal politics, and potentially to gain a sphere of influence in Somalia, the site of a simmering proxy war with Eritrea. There were regular, unconfirmed reports of Ethiopian troop movements inside Somalia, but the presence had remained rather a lurking one, and the Ethiopian government was prone to denying that its troops were there at all.

Islamist fighters, meanwhile, were said to be moving in the direction of Baidoa, attempting to expand their area of control. Heavy fighting began on 19

December. Six days later, Ethiopia, stacitly supported by the US, conducted air strikes on Mogadishu airport. (Washington fears the potential spread of militant Islam through the Horn of Africa, and believes that jihadist elements within the ICU are shielding those responsible for the 1998 bombing of US embassies in Nairobi and Dar es Salaam.) By 27 December the Ethiopians had taken control of several key towns, including Jowhar, and were closing in on Mogadishu. The *Times Online* reported that the famed warlord Mohammed Dheere – who used to run Jowhar – had returned in triumph wearing an 'I love Jowhar' T-shirt.

No one had foreseen how rapidly power would shift and the speed with which the Islamic Courts would evaporate. In our own 'contingency planning' exercises – which mapped out possible political scenarios and their expected effects on the humanitarian situation – we had deemed a 'protracted stand-off' between the TFG and the ICU as the most likely scenario for the coming months.

As TFG and Ethiopian troops consolidated their control over much of South/Central, ICU forces retreated south, to Lower Juba. On 8 January, from its military base in Djibouti, the US launched an air strike on Lower Juba, targeting an area near the border with Kenya where ICU forces were thought to be hiding. There were unconfirmed reports of casualties among the nomadic population, and local communities reported significant livestock losses. By then, Kenya had sealed its border with Somalia, meaning that the mass exodus of refugees our contingency planning had predicted (in the 'worst-case scenario' of widespread conflict) did not come to pass; instead, there were four thousand Somalis stranded at the border. Humanitarian operations in South/Central came to a virtual halt.

Many residents of Mogadishu initially welcomed the installation of the TFG. The ICU had clamped down on khat-trading, an economic mainstay of the capital, and the increasing domination by the more radical wing of the Courts was viewed by many with apprehension. The UN welcomed the TFG too. Although the moderates within the ICU had seemed genuinely committed to working with the humanitarian community, the extremist element was problematic and there was a lack of clarity about who was calling which shots. Now, although the TFG was in place only through Ethiopian support – or occupation – at least the internationally recognized government and the people controlling access to the populations in need were one and the same, simplifying the picture. Or so we thought.

Following two high-level UN missions to Mogadishu during the second week in January, my office issued a press release in which we announced that the international aid community 'must take immediate advantage of the window of opportunity that now exists in Somalia by substantially re-engaging in the capital'. It was hoped that by quickly implementing 'high-impact projects' that would make immediate and visible changes in people's lives, humanitarian organizations could support stabilization and prevent a power vacuum from forming. There was talk of finally relocating the humanitarian operation from Nairobi to Somalia.

The press release ruffled many feathers, particularly within the international NGOs, as many felt that what we were calling a 'window of opportunity' was in fact a highly dangerous and unpredictable situation. Meanwhile, very few people I knew in Nairobi – including myself – wanted the operation to relocate to Somalia.

Although what we referred to as 'major hostilities' ceased in early January, other forms of violence almost immediately surfaced – or resurfaced – in Mogadishu. As the early months of 2007 wore on, the situation in the city went from 'unpredictable' and 'erratic' – what it was hoped was simply the dust settling after the change in personnel – to 'deteriorating' (the security) and 'escalating' (the violence).

Calls by the TFG for freelance militias to disarm went largely unheeded. House-to-house searches began, triggering gun battles in the streets. There were mortar and rocket-propelled-grenade attacks on the city's seaport, airport, presidential palace and various neighbourhoods. For months, we avoided using the word 'insurgency' in our reports, referring instead to 'anti-TFG factions'; at some point, and without there seeming to have been any discussion on the matter, we began to write of an 'insurgency'. Several government-appointed officials and their close associates were assassinated. Ethiopian convoys and TFG troops were targeted. The Ethiopian response to attacks was often to fire indiscriminately in the general direction from which they had come. Every day, civilians were dying in the crossfire. Elders in some Mogadishu neighbourhoods began to form vigilante squads, and gunmen were reportedly being hired for $2 a day.

Checkpoints and roadblocks, which had disappeared in many areas of South/Central under the ICU, began to spring up again, and reports of looting, banditry, extortion, harassment and rape were all on the rise. In Mogadishu, the brief period in which the capital's citizens had moved through the city with relative freedom was over. Meanwhile, people were dying of acute watery diarrhoea.

About 8,000 African Union peacekeeping troops were pledged by countries including Nigeria, Burundi, Malawi and Ghana, but only 1,600, from Uganda, showed up; as of November 2007, they remain the only AU troops in Somalia. Their presence did nothing to quell the violence, though it was mainly the Ethiopians who were targeted by the insurgency. Although their stated intention had been to withdraw within weeks of having defeated the ICU, the Ethiopians had remained and were increasingly seen as an army of occupation; the more indiscriminately they used their weaponry in Mogadishu's residential areas, the more unpopular they grew. On 21 March, in a nifty allusion to the events of 1993, when the bodies of US soldiers were dragged through the streets of Mogadishu, militia fighters dragged the bodies of five TFG and Ethiopian soldiers through the streets of Mogadishu. Then they burned them.

In my weekly reports, I was running out of ways to say that things were getting worse. The opening line of the Friday sitrep was always a variation on: *The security situation in Mogadishu deteriorated, with violence and insecurity escalating. Mortar and RPG attacks, gun battles and targeted assassinations continued. Thousands more have fled the city …*

At about five o'clock on 23 March, having filed the Friday sitrep and logged off, and while waiting for the elevator, I got a call from my boss telling me a plane had just been shot down over Mogadishu and people were dead. We needed to send an email to New York about this. I rolled my eyes and turned back toward the office, realizing as I did that I too had begun to suffer from Somalia fatigue. I was tired of thinking about Somalia and its circular, repetitive, self-defeating dramas.

On the back of a piece of paper (recycled office paper containing someone's flight itinerary to Masai Mara), I scribbled:

> *chartered plane for AU private co*
> *AU was bringing in plane w/ 11 people*
> *Belarus Co*
> *e/o died*
> *missile or RPG*
> *not UN plane*
> *15km from Int A'port*

The following day, I got a call on my mobile from someone named Vladimir in a UN office in Minsk. It was about the plane or, more specifically, the eleven bodies. Belarus, through its Permanent Mission in New York, was seeking security guarantees from the African Union for safe passage of the bodies and whoever would fly in to remove them. (Their concern was understandable; those killed the previous day had been travelling to Mogadishu to repair another plane that had been hit by a rocket-propelled grenade the week before.) But African Union forces could not guarantee safe passage. They weren't the ones shooting down planes.

There was also the question of the heat. Special 'cellophane packets' were needed to protect the bodies from decay while they awaited relocation from Mogadishu airport to what Vladimir called 'the Motherland'.

I wanted to help Vladimir, possibly as much as I had wanted to help anyone in my ten months with the UN. Maybe it was because Vladimir's problem was, relative to other Somalia-related problems, fairly straightforward, one my office might actually be able to help solve. But it was also something about Vladimir himself, the way he spoke – his heart-rending Eastern-bloc English – and his courtly, archaic prose style, with which I became familiar in the coming days. Vladimir wrote things like: *I will avail myself, with your permission, of the opportunity to render your kind assistance once again …*

The following week, with the help of the African Union and our staff in Mogadishu, the bodies were safely evacuated, and Vladimir and I exchanged an electronic handshake at the conclusion of what he termed this 'sad and sensitive' affair.

Meanwhile, throughout the month of April, *violence and insecurity escalated in Mogadishu, with mortar and RPG attacks, gun battles and targeted assassinations on the increase …*

Despite the downward spiral, the TFG declared victory. A 26 April headline on SomaliNet read:

Somalia PM says mission accomplished

The headline referred to the government's claim that troops had ousted the remaining insurgents from the capital and that 'stability will be restored to normalcy'. The headline was replete with meaning. It served as reminder, first, of the fact that the TFG and the Ethiopians were in bed with America and, second, of what quagmires await those in the grip of hubris. It was steeped in the self-mockery and irony which are the stock in trade of Somalis. And there was that Somali conceit too – that while the Americans might have been dumb enough to believe their leader when he said the same about Iraq, they knew better.

I reported the TFG's claim as well. Our sitrep of 27 April read:

Following several days of fierce fighting in Mogadishu in which TFG/Ethiopian forces exchanged heavy artillery and gunfire with anti-government factions, the TFG is claiming to have taken control of much of the city. There have been reports of widespread looting. The TFG claim comes at the end of an intensely violent week. A car bomb exploded on 24 April outside the Ambassador Hotel, a base for Somali lawmakers, reportedly killing seven civilians. A second car bomb, a possible suicide attack, exploded outside an Ethiopian military base 30 km from the city on the road to Afgoye. The headquarters of local NGO DBG (Daryeel Bulsho Guud) was hit during the week, reportedly injuring agency staff, while on 26 April, SOS children's and maternity hospital was struck by mortars, reportedly resulting in the death of several patients. The hospital was closed and all staff evacuated. Civilians have continued to flee Mogadishu, with the latest estimate of displacement standing at 365,000. Residents are reporting that sections of the city are almost entirely deserted.

Clearly, the 'window of opportunity' had shut, though the phrase had not been forgotten by those in Nairobi-Somalia. It had come to symbolize the UN's capacity for self-delusion and wishful thinking. But the jokes were growing old. Obstructionist and often absurd, the TFG had become everyone's worst nightmare. On the day we issued the above report, Prime Minister Gedi was quoted in the *Times* of London accusing UN agencies of using private airstrips to ship in contraband, weapons and insurgents; of striking deals with warlords and the ousted ICU and pocketing the proceeds. 'They want to operate in this country without any control,' Gedi said. 'They know they can't do that any more ... Now there's a Prime Minister who knows them too well.'

The UN was also accused of exaggerating the scale of the crisis. While we said 365,000 people had been displaced by the violence, the TFG claimed the figure was only 40,000. Reports of human rights violations committed by TFG and Ethiopian troops were piling up. Humanitarian workers were being harassed, threatened and arrested. Gedi publicly accused the World Food Programme of causing a health crisis (between January and June there would be 40,000 cases of cholera or acute watery diarrhoea in South/Central, resulting in an estimated 1,133 deaths) by distributing spoiled food rations. Even the US, with its anyone-but-the-Islamists mantra, was becoming exasperated. In a BBC interview, US Assistant Secretary of State for African Affairs Jendayi Frazer said that it was 'difficult to frankly say' that Somalia was currently better off than it had been before the Ethiopian intervention.

8

My year-long contract to report on Somalia had ended in June, but in August I returned to the Office for the Coordination of Humanitarian Affairs in Nairobi for four months to write the annual Consolidated Appeal on behalf of all UN agencies and several NGOs implementing projects in Somalia. The document, aimed at donor countries and organizations, seeks funding for about 150 emergency relief projects and provides a narrative of events in Somalia over the previous year. By August, as seems always to be the case with Somalia, much had happened but very little had changed.

Although the insurgency was gaining in strength, the TFG had finally managed to stage its thrice-postponed National Reconciliation Conference (NRC) in Mogadishu. The stated purpose of the conference was to launch a political process that would eventually create a national accord for the peaceful governance of all Somalia's clans and political groupings. Controversially, President

Yusuf had organized the conference on the basis of clan membership rather than political divisions. (Yusuf is from the Darod clan, the long-time adversary of Mogadishu's dominant Hawiye clan, which supported the Islamic Courts.) Opposition groups based in Eritrea – the political wing of the ICU, dissident members of the TFG parliament, nationalists opposed to a clan-based formula for Somalia, sectors of the Somali diaspora, and some ex-warlords – had boycotted the conference on the grounds that selecting delegates on the basis of clan allowed the TFG to evade serious power-sharing negotiations. Many had refused to consider a conference held in Somalia as long as the country remained under Ethiopian occupation. In the absence of so many key constituencies, the significance of two of the conference's stated achievements – a clan cease-fire and disarmament, and the restoration of properties stolen during clan conflicts – is questionable: no mechanisms for monitoring or enforcement were put in place and, as of November, no progress had been made on either issue. On hte other hand, the fact that the NRC was able to take place at all is seen by some to indicate that substantial segments of Somali society are willing to give reconciliation a chance and to engage in a political process

The opposition groups that had boycotted the NRC gathered in September in Asmara. The Somali Congress for Liberation and Reconstitution succeeded only in agreeing on the need to remove Ethiopian forces from Somalia. The ICU continued to insist on a Somalia ruled by Shari'a law, while dissident parliamentarians and diaspora groups favoured wider democratic power-sharing with the TFG (subject to an Ethiopian withdrawal). The nationalists, who pulled out of the Congress (citing fears that the it would be dominated by the ICU and that no 'post-liberation vision' would result), favour a non-theocratic state transcending clan divisions.

Meanwhile, things have not got better for the people of Somalia. A combination of the large-scale displacement from the latest conflict (450,000 people estimated to have fled Mogadishu between January and November 2007) and the poor performance of the spring rains have resulted in a 50 per cent increase since early 2007 in the number of people the UN terms 'in need of assistance and protection'. This figure of 1.5 million includes 750,000 people either in 'Acute Food & Livelihood Crisis' or 'Humanitarian Emergency'. An estimated 83,000 children are suffering from acute malnutrition. Twenty-five per cent of children in South/Central have stunted growth as a result of malnutrition. There are close to two hundred checkpoints or roadblocks in South/Central, delaying aid deliveries for days and creating all the usual nightmares for the local population. In December, the UN – through its Consolidated Appeal – will ask donors for over $370 million for humanitarian assistance in 2008. One of the projects for which funding is sought has a $1,000,000 budget to cover vocational training for young boys. It's not easy for an NGO to compete in Mogadishu's labour market. Currently, the insurgents are said to be paying kids $100 a pop to lob grenades at Ethiopians.

Purity of diction in English verse

IAN SANSOM

I went up, as they say, to Cambridge just over twenty years ago, in 1986, and all of the usual clichés applied: I was the first person in my family ever to attend university; I came from a comprehensive school; I came from Essex; I felt sorry for myself; I felt I didn't fit in; I became ill and overwrought, and had to take time off to recover; I fell in love; I went travelling, to find myself, and found I wasn't there; I lost my religion; and worse, I completely lost my sense of humour. It was, I suppose, like most things in life, totally unoriginal and stereotypical: three years of confused and straining emotions, and intense, overdramatized intellectual activity, accompanied by endless instant coffee and Leonard Cohen.

I remember arriving at the college and walking through the big carved wooden gates with my rucksack and my carrier bags and being amazed at the sight of all the trunks lined up outside the porter's lodge. I had no idea people actually owned trunks. I'd never seen an actual trunk before, a trunk in the flesh, as it were. You didn't get trunks where I was from: we had hold-alls. I thought trunks were just props in Sunday-night BBC costume dramas, like elephant-foot umbrella stands and tiger-skin rugs. Going to university felt like going to New York for the first time: it felt as though I wasn't there, and yet as if I'd been there all my life. I'd gone to a place that existed in my head.

It was a dream come true. I attended lectures every day – went to everything, even to lectures and seminars on subjects I knew nothing about and wasn't interested in – and stayed up late every night reading, got up early to read, read right through the weekends and the holidays, never ever went out to eat, and maybe drank a pint of beer a week, maximum, to relax. It was all those books everywhere – they turned my head. I just couldn't believe it was happening to me. I had grown up in a house with a dictionary and a big red *Children's Britannica* paid for in instalments, and I had exhausted my local library years before, and now, to be released into the English Faculty Library and the college library, and the University Library, it was like placing a starving man in an all-you-can-eat Chinese restaurant during National Eating Out For Free Week, or putting a rat in a laboratory cage crammed full with trapdoors and tidbits, and I suffered and enjoyed all of the predictable indulgences and agonies of the apprentice intellectual: hubris, pride, arrogance, bloating, self-doubt and self-disgust. The late nineteen-eighties were the years of the Iran–Iraq war, and Exocet missiles, and the Piper Alpha disaster, and the rise of Solidarity in Poland, and yet just about all I can remember of world events is the day of the Lockerbie air crash – because I went to see *Cinema Paradiso*. Or was it *Babette's Feast* and the Iran-Contra affair? The years run into each other and blur. I had become a first-class solipsist. I was a pig in shit.

Before arriving in Cambridge I'd been working as an evangelist, living with church families, preaching the Word day and night, so having my own room with a single gas ring was the first chance I'd had to be alone and to think for myself and eat toast by myself for a very long time. I had a room with big windows – the nicest room I've ever had, before or since, a single room at least the size if not bigger than any of the bedsit flats I lived in later during my twenties – and going up the stone steps to that room was like entering a monastery, or being on spiritual retreat. I spent an hour each morning praying and studying the Bible and then I would go to breakfast in the upper dining hall, as soon as it opened, and talk to the chaplain and to a couple of foreign students – the only other people up and about early – and then I'd cycle off to the Sidgwick site, which reminded me not unpleasantly of Harlow, or of Basildon, and so which seemed like home, and there I would take up my books again, with no discernible difference in my public attentions towards, say, *The Faerie Queene* than in my private devotions to the Scriptures.

The atmosphere in the Cambridge English Faculty has of course always been rather churchy; when I ended up in Oxford years later I couldn't believe it when I saw and heard dons on the job laughing and smiling. Didn't these people realize they were dealing with sacred texts, with *English Literature*? In Cambridge I clearly recall the curate-like super-structuralist Stephen Heath wearing a black turtleneck and giving lectures on F.R. Leavis and Puritan v. Puritan, and Geoffrey Hill coming on like an Old Testament prophet, or maybe more like some evil cardinal from the TV adaptation of Colleen McCullough's *The Thorn Birds*. Hill ran a seminar series on the First World War poets and I remember I went along for the first session, sitting in silence with the other supplicants, and Hill storming in and slamming down his big black bag on the desk and starting to speak straight away, off-the-cuff, no notes, and without so much as a by-your-leave. At the time I found it terrifying, but later, when I became briefly and unsuccessfully an academic myself, I realized that a lot of what appeared to be pure, raw intellectual power was in fact just high-class bravura and play-acting: if it wasn't exactly camp then there was certainly a large amount of vamp.

I set about my study of Literature in much the same way as I set about my study of the Bible – I read, I marked, and I inwardly digested. I made long lists of books I had to read, and ticked them off once I'd read them: Shakespeare, tick; Dickens, tick; Proust, half a tick; *The Great Tradition*, tick; *Purity of Diction in English Verse*, tick; *The Sense of an Ending*, tick. I filled page after A4-narrow-feint-with-margin page with my notes. Every essay was hand-written, once, twice, sometimes dozens of times (no one I knew back then had a computer, and that was only twenty years ago, so you can imagine what's going to happen in the future: students delivering essays by telepathy, and subcutaneous barcoding to record credits and debits on their student loans). In addition to the set texts and recommended reading I read poetry and novels by exciting young writers like Paul Muldoon and Graham Swift, and just about anything else that took my fancy – Freud one week, Kierkegaard the next, Dante, Lewis Mumford, Levinas, Ruskin, Adorno. I didn't care whether they were dead or alive,

French, German, Italian, or who or what the hell they were: I just wanted to know. I read literary criticism like it was going out of fashion, which it may well have done for all I know. I must have read *Darwin's Plots* by Gillian Beer and *The Force of Poetry* by Christopher Ricks about a dozen times. I discovered John Berryman as a critic in his book *The Freedom of the Poet*, and I read all of Empson also, and they became my heroes, because they were just about the only critics I could find with anything like a sense of humour, or a sense of the ridiculous. Literary criticism, I later came to realize, is an activity often undertaken by people with rather grandiose and sentimental ideas about human civilization and about their role and importance to it, but I don't think I noticed this at the time, or at least it didn't bother me, because I had some pretty grandiose and sentimental ideas about human civilization and my role and importance to it myself.

My unacknowledged aim and intention at Cambridge, I think, was to gain an education – not in the broadest sense, because I felt I'd already had an education in the broadest sense. I didn't need any more life experiences, I'd had quite enough of that: what I needed were books. I steered clear of girls, and drink, and parties, and all other possible distractions. I did not play sport, or attend concerts (I did play in a band, but that's another story). Before arriving in Cambridge my idea of listening to difficult music was putting on my cassette of *The Name of This Band Is Talking Heads*, but I knew that I needed to broaden my horizons, and so I started listening to Radio 3, jotting down names and titles of music that I needed to learn to appreciate: 'Brook's Violin Concerto'; 'Sibelius, No. 5'; 'Marler'. Until I was nineteen I don't think I'd ever heard any classical music at all, unless by accident – I have a vague memory of *The Planets* suite from primary school. I'd certainly never been to an art gallery. So I had a lot of catching up to do. I went to the Fitzwilliam Museum to look at the paintings and occasionally, if I had the money, I'd go down to London to an exhibition. I was a culture vulture. I was an insufferable prig.

I don't know how the supervision system works in Cambridge these days, but back in the 1980s a lot of the teaching was farmed out to graduate students and to young Research Fellows – so, at eighteen or nineteen, you might end up being taught by people who were just two or three years older than you, which was unnerving, both for you and, presumably, for them. There was a giddying, half-sensed possibility that you might actually know more about a particular book or author than your friendly fresh-faced mentor and guide. (Indeed, I know this must often have been the case, because a few years later, as a graduate student at Oxford, I did some undergraduate teaching myself and, desperate for the money, I agreed to teach anything – Medieval, Renaissance, Eighteenth-century, Women's Travel Writing, subjects about which I knew next to nothing – and I remember staying up one night reading Tennyson in preparation for the next day's tutorials, and somehow bluffing my way through on the strength of Christoper Ricks' critical edition and a couple of memorized verses of 'In Memoriam'.) It all seems incredibly amateurish, looking back on it – a bodge-and-patch kind of ivory tower, like some Heath Robinson cartoon. Photocopied sheets would arrive in your pigeonhole from your Director of Studies, informing you of the name and address of this or that supervisor, and you'd have to look up the address on the big map in the porter's lodge, and then you'd have to cycle out there at the appointed hour, and knock sheepishly on the door, to be met by a complete stranger, and in you'd go, paperback Dickens in hand, ready to have your mind carefully honed by the use of the Socratic method and by the example of your fellow students showing off and trying to outwit you. There are doubtless better ways of preparing young people for adult life, but there are also probably worse. (Some of my friends from school had joined the army and I'd been a spit away from doing so myself – I'd filled in the forms, but chickened out at the last minute and never took them back to the recruiting office.) Sometimes the supervisors had college rooms, but more often they did not, and you'd be cycling out to neat little terraced houses in chi-chi Cambridge suburbs, full of books and stripped pine floors, and it was unnerving: I'd never seen a stripped pine floor before, and there was occasionally a disturbing hint of a wife or children hovering somewhere in the background while we sat around and talked about *Ulysses*, or *Krapp's Last Tape*, and I could never work out how these people combined the life of the mind with their lives as fathers and husbands; I still can't work it out now, as a matter of fact, as a father and husband myself; I don't know how they did it. It was like going to visit a very wealthy, very worldly, and very wise older brother. (We were never supervised by a woman.)

There were three or four supervisors during my time as an undergraduate in Cambridge who made a big impression on me. There was a man called Chris Bristow, who supervised us for the Part II Tragedy paper (the ins and outs of the Cambridge Tripos examination system, like the doctrine of the Holy Trinity, I never fully understood, even when as a Research Fellow some years later I was supposed to be preparing students for it myself). For the fabled Tragedy paper Chris Bristow's reading list, which I still have, began 'You should read as many as possible of the 33 extant plays of Aeschylus, Sophocles and Euripides', so I did, and not only the University of Chicago Press editions, but also the H.D.F. Kitto translations, and the Robert Fagles. As well as the Greeks and Shakespeare, Chris – 'Call me Chris', he said, without guile, so we did – suggested we should read Wittgenstein, and Stanley Cavell, and Kierkegaard, authors who have remained favourites and companions ever since. I still have all my notes for the Tragedy paper – I have them right here in front of me, kept for years in the proverbial manila folder, marked 'TRAGEDY' (I also still have my 'SHAKESPEARE', and my 'POPE', and my 'PRAC CRIT', and a much slimmer folder, containing some leaflets about joining the Civil Service, titled, optimistically, 'CAREERS'). My actual notes are unremarkable, in a big fat biro hand, but I was at least thorough, noting down title, author, date and place of publication, and also the shelfmark in red at the top-right corner of each page, so even now I could tell you where to find books on the shelves of the old English Faculty library, just in case you needed to know: 701.15.c.95; 180.c.97.877; 9180.d.3230.

I loved the Tragedy paper. I loved all the Tripos papers, to be honest – 'The History and Theory of Literary Criticism.' 'English Literature and its Background, 1830–Present Day', even the specious 'Special Topics' ('Money' and 'Kingship' I recall). But I loved the Tragedy paper the best, and I loved it because of Chris's suggested essay questions, which were quite unlike the questions we were usually asked to consider for other papers, quite unlike, say, 'In the following pairing (b) is a later version of (a). To what extent, if at all, could it be considered an improvement?', or 'Fielding's moral intensity. Discuss'. The questions for the Tragedy paper – and again I still have the list, typewritten rather than word-processed – these are questions I would still dearly love to have answers for. 'Why do we want to watch presentations of grief, pain and disaster?' 'Under what aspects or pressures does history become destiny?' And my absolute favourite, 'What ways of describing tragedy can you think of that would definitely exclude comedy?' (Answer to this last: none.)

I was also taught by someone called Steve Xerri. He taught us French – a good reading knowledge of a foreign language being regarded as essential for all students studying Eng. Lit. back then, as it may properly still be today. A good command of a foreign language seemed not to be a problem for most people, many of whom seemed to be half-French anyway, or who had at least been to France, but I had only a CSE in French and a school day-trip to Calais under my belt, and those weekly sessions with unseen translations and Sartre's *Les Mots* were for me the toughest part of the Tripos; everything else was a breeze in comparison, even the dreaded Dating paper (in which you were asked to identify the date and if possible even the author of a piece of writing from internal stylistic clues alone: could it be Malory? could be Chaucer? could it perhaps be Tom Paine?). About all I could manage in French was to order a ham sandwich, and then ask for the bill and find out the time of the next train, *s'il vous plaît*, and now here I was being expected to read *Les Misérables*. Steve put me in the equivalent of the slow learner's group, and took us slowly through bits of Balzac and poems by Baudelaire and somehow coached us through. I recall him being extraordinarily patient and he was also an artist, I think, when he wasn't teaching us French vocabulary: he used to make collages, big Russian Futurist/John Heartfield-influenced kind of things, which were displayed on the walls, and he dressed all in black, and his partner, another Steve, taught us the nineteenth-century novel down in the basement of their house. The two Steves were not, as far as I know, attached to any particular college – indeed, all of the supervisors who impressed me in Cambridge were slightly peripheral to the main business going on in the colleges. The college-based supervisors tended to be older and weirder, or just plain alcoholics full of cellar sherry and self-loathing, although there were some notable exceptions: there was a man called Fred Parker, for example, who supervised my dissertation on the poet William Cowper, and a young bloke called Peter Swaab, who liked Talking Heads and The Gang of Four. And there was also a poet – an actual poet – Peter Robinson.

I'd heard about Peter Robinson long before he became my supervisor. I used to attend the lectures given by Eric Griffiths on practical criticism. Everyone used to attend the lectures given by Eric Griffiths on practical criticism. Maybe they still do, if he's still going. I remember Griffiths as a great showman, brooding and begowned, the master of the simple prop, like a priest with the host, or a character in a play by Beckett; with just his native wit, and a beaker of water, and a few photocopied handouts, he was able to hold your attention for an hour without your mind wandering too far beyond the confines of the tower-block-type lecture theatre to the world beyond; for an hour, you could imagine that this really was all that mattered: the curious little ambiguities and the meaningful small things, the author's profound sleights of hand and acts of mind. I can still see the rimless-spectacled Dr Griffiths exactly in my mind's eye, up the front, with his salt-and-pepper hair and his 1980s casual-structured jacket, handing out his photocopied sheets of minutely-typed excerpts of poetry and prose, and him taking a meaningful sip at his water – this was work! – and then starting in on all that lovely Literature, piece by tiny piece, like a gastronome settling down to some huge seafood platter: scraps of Shakespeare prised open, little bits of Browning, collops of Hopkins or Ashbery. And there, one week, as he waded in among all of the white meat and shards was a poem by someone none of us had ever heard of: Peter Robinson. Whether Griffiths mentioned the fact that Robinson was alive and well and young and teaching in Cambridge or whether the rumour went round afterwards I don't know. But I do know that the next time I was in Heffer's Bookshop – and I was in Heffer's bookshop just about every day then, browsing and spending the money I saved from only ever eating the subsidized meals in college and working on farms and in quarries during the holidays – I bought copies of this poet Robinson's slim volumes, *Overdrawn Account* (1980) and *Anaglypta* (1985).

My pencilled notes and annotations seem to indicate that I first started reading the poems sometime in 1987, and that I was stopped short by the first poem in *Anaglypta*, '472 Claremont Road', and by the very first lines, which are a quotation from T.S. Eliot quoting I.A. Richards, I believe:

> 'Poetry "is capable of saving us", he says;
> it is like saying that the wall-paper will
> Save us when the walls have crumbled.'

This caught my attention, obviously, as a religious maniac turned culture-worshipper who was rapidly losing faith even in the saving powers of literature. So, I liked the epigraph, and I also liked the title of the poem, which seemed like a real address, in a real city or suburb, which was a good start after years of having to study poems at school with titles like 'Anahorish' and 'Crow Hill', which might as well have been signposted to Mars for anyone from suburban Essex. And then of course I liked what he did in the actual poem – playing with ideas of surfaces and depths, and paper and memory, and his describing a derelict house, and how the wallpaper might indeed still be hanging when the walls were tumbling down:

> Then
>
> anaglypta, the word is, hung on while
> brick or plaster, whatever the thing was,
> gave to my touch: like digestive biscuit
> crumbled under packaging.

I liked the word – the insistence on the correct, slightly ludicrous, undignified trade and domestic word – 'anaglypta' and I also liked the image of the crumbled digestive biscuit, which I underlined, and which I suppose must have struck me somehow as a clinching metaphor, evidence that here was someone who had a grasp of the real world, of the mundane and everyday, a grasp that I'd been reaching out for and failing to find in the dozens of books of contemporary poetry I was reading, finding most of it far too flashy, too wowsy, or too clumsy and rough for my tastes. I liked them, then, from the very first; the intelligence, the obvious sympathies, and also the avowed modesty of the poems.

I liked the poet also, as it turned out. I had never before met a poet, or a writer of any kind. I had no inkling that any good poets might still be alive: the only good poets I'd ever come across were dead. I'd assumed that all actual living poets would be like Roger McGough or Adrian Henri, who I didn't really care for because they seemed like they didn't really want to be poets; they really wanted to be pop stars; and the pop stars were better at being pop stars, so why bother? Peter Robinson, it turned out, was not interested in being a pop star. He first supervised me, I think, during my second year at Cambridge, and I recall thinking that he wasn't that much older than me, and I recall also that he always wore a round-neck sweater and soft leather shoes, and I vaguely remember the house he was teaching in – did he own the house? was he borrowing it during the daytime? I have no idea; all I remember is that it was near a cemetery.

I have notes from the supervisions, which don't really amount to much, and are more likely to be my interpretation of our conversations than quotations of anything he actually said: 'D.H. Lawrence, an odd man'; 'Calm is complex'; 'Only partial clarifications'; 'Poetry and the human project'. But I also have my old essays, with his careful markings in which, with an uncanny kind of prescience, he seems to get exactly at what my writing would become: 'You stop just in time, with the world of Woody Allen and colour supplement writing pretentiously round the corner.' Ah, yes. Another essay, though, ends, 'Excellent: accurate, strenuous and imaginative. Well done you,' which was a fillip, and there were numerous other encouragements.

It transpired or emerged, or somehow was revealed, that Peter had edited poetry magazines and been involved in the Cambridge Poetry Festivals, which seemed enormously glamorous to me, and which may have planted the idea in my head to have a go and do the same. When I became involved, years later, in a poetry magazine called *Thumbscrew* and sent Peter a copy, he replied promptly with a postcard. I still have the postcard. It reads, judiciously, 'I've just read the whole thing from cover to cover and found nothing much to dislike.' This seems to me to be a perfect sentence, from one end to the other, not merely rhythmically but also in that sure-footed combination of empathy and objectivity; and at least he read, or pretended to read, the bloody thing, which is more than most people did.

The importance of the careful choice of words, *whether or not anyone else is ever going to read them* – that's one of the things I began to understand in Cambridge. I also began to appreciate that literary criticism can be an art form in itself, in the hands of its greatest exponents, but that it requires the kind of patience and bloody-mindedness that has to be devoted to the making of any work of art, and that if you skimp it, it shows. Years later, when I'd published a few things myself, on W.H. Auden, Peter took me to task in print. I deserved it. My criticism was wayward and impressionistic – associative and undisciplined – and I slowly realized that I did not possess the necessary determination and skills to become a great literary critic, and that what little powers I did possess I would need to further my other little endeavours, attempts to write serious sorts of books that don't necessarily signal their seriousness and so which might, in an ideal world, appeal both to connoisseurs of literature and to others, to my younger self, and to my better self, to Essex, and to Cambridge.

The pleasant light of day

PHILIP Ó CEALLAIGH

The man had looked at a map and figured it was a simple walk from the hotel to the museum. Now he observed the alien script of the street signs and shop signs which could not even be resolved into individual letters and heard snatches of strange speech as the faces passed at speed. He was conscious of the maleness of the street, the few women scarved and overdressed in the warm weather. He held his son's hand. It was early morning and the boy's mother was still drowsing in her bed.

His son, five years old, was silent now and very serious at the task of getting down the street. The boy had never seen so many people. The noise of the car horns and the intense traffic made it difficult for them to speak. The boy was usually very talkative. He was very good with words, and when he did not understand a word he would ask what it meant.

For example, once the man had taken him to fish from the rocks at home and the boy had soon become bored. 'You don't have patience,' he told him.

'What's patience?'

He had thought for a moment and then replied: 'Patience is giving to each thing the time you need to do it well. So, to fish, you need patience, until the fish comes to you.'

Later that day he asked the boy what patience was, and the boy replied immediately: 'Waiting.'

Or, when they had been collecting bait, using stones to whack limpets off rocks, the boy, who loved animals, asked, 'Doesn't it hurt them?'

'Fish bait. They're history.'

'What's history?'

He thought about this. He liked the process of taking a word apart in order to explain an idea simply. It helped him notice the natural connection between ideas. And, like holding the boy's hand, explaining words gave him a place in the world. He delivered simple blocks of meaning, and watched the boy play with them, turning them around as he would solid objects, examining them for use. He observed the boy's world growing, branching out in fresh directions, as he gathered words.

'History is something that has happened, and you tell a story about it.'

'So. It's a story. That's real.'

'Yes, but when I say "They're history" I just mean, that's it, the story is over for them, the end.'

The boy, sitting on his hunkers on the wet sand, pondering history by the tide pool, nodded, his mouth a little open.

Later, the boy shouted across the waves 'You're history!' as the man cast a hook baited with a struggling worm. The father laughed, the wind and the sun in his face. In such moments he felt that children were geniuses in a bright new world, one that only later grew dim. He wanted to hold the boy's hand a little longer, while he still belonged to such a world. Growing older, people found dull ways to make life bearable. Or perhaps did not find any way.

And now they were walking down a strange street, with the traffic screaming, and the traffic cop at the intersection whistling, to the Egyptian Museum of Antiquities.

They reached a 'square', a vast open space where vehicles converged from a number of busy streets, and they stopped and stood there together, looking across, holding hands, as if they had reached the shore of a sea. There was no place to cross. Cars swarmed about each other like ants on an anthill, somehow avoiding collision. It was very loud. The sounds of the horns rose above the sound of the engines. They watched and the boy waited for the next thing his father would do. The father could see people crossing, passing between moving lanes of traffic as if protected by magic charms. But he did not have the nerve for such a trick, and certainly not with a child. Then he saw the sign for the metro station and the people going down into the ground.

The man and the boy descended into the tunnels beneath the square. The tunnels branched and turned many times. They went up and down stairs. The man saw signs in Arabic that he could not read and signs in Latin script indicating streets he did not know.

'Dad, do you know the way?'

'Approximately.'

'What's approximately?'

'Kind of.'

When they came up again to the sky and the square they were closer to the museum and there were no more big roads to cross.

'They have a really lot of cars in Cairo, Dad.'

'They do.'

'How many do they have, would you say?'

'A lot a lot.'

'But how many really, Dad?'

'Oh, millions.'

'That's a really lot! Why don't they crash?'

'I don't know. I think they do. Sometimes.'

The museum was located in a street that was blocked off to general traffic. Only police and military vehicles and tour buses were admitted. There were ordinary police, soldiers and riot police with shields. Soldiers stood guard behind blast shields.

'Why are there soldiers, Dad?'

It was a police state, for one thing. It had made peace with Israel and received American money in return, and had developed a tourist industry, the only real industry there was, and this investment had to be protected against bombers and their deadly shrapnel.

'To keep an eye on things.'

'What things, like?'

'Crazy runaway crocodiles, from the river Nile.'

The boy smiled. They were away from the traffic now, with the tourists and the soldiers, and it was easier to speak.

'Have their guns got bullets, Dad? Real ones?'

'I'd say so.'

They entered the main gates in front of the museum and he bought tickets and declined the services of several guides. They had a brief rest, sitting outside talking, about crocodiles and hippopotamuses mainly, and then they entered one of the greatest museums on earth.

The Egyptian Museum of Antiquities fairly represented the country, the man felt. A musty deposit of wonders, a coffin shop, a sarcophagus warehouse. The exhibits were crowded and jumbled. Those in cases were described in Arabic and English by small cards bearing the clunky font of an old typewriter, the English a mess of stylistic, grammatical and typographical errors, comically slapdash in a museum with a grand name implying respect for the sciences.

The chaos of the city had pervaded the museum.

They wandered from case to case, stopping when an exhibit held the boy's attention and gave them something to discuss, and he explained what he could. But the boy was interested in ordinary household objects, things that he could easily recognize. Objects so banal that it seemed strange that they should be exhibited at all. Looking at such things with his son, the man felt that the world of the past was as real as that in which he lived, though glimpsed through the odd distorting glass of a museum display-case. It was not the world of the dead that seemed strange to him, but the dead analytical impulse that had removed the objects from the living hands that had held and used them, from rooms where families had lived and children grown up, and had put them in display cases as if they were extraordinary. They were not extraordinary. It was just that the people who had used them had been gone a long time.

As he walked the corridors of the dead he could not shake the mad hum of the city outside. He had a sudden vertiginous sensation that the living city was just one more layer superimposed upon all the dead layers. All the motion, joy, excitement going on outside – a fly buzzing blind against a windowpane.

He looked at simple functional objects such as pots and knives and sandals, and then looked up and saw the tourists performing their stations, and it was the tourists who made the least sense. What strange species of people needed to look at such things as though they were hard to understand? There was even a chunk of ancient bread on display. Preserved in the dry air of a tomb, it now resembled a rock. But what was bread when it was no longer for eating? And what kind of a human being needed to look at bread that was no longer bread, but bread for looking at in a case, and yet needed to be told 'This is bread'?

He had had a similar feeling several days before, on the plane, looking at the ancient desert through gaps in the unreal-looking clouds, thinking what an improbable thing it was to fly, to sail above the earth in a metal bird, ignorant of how the trick worked, and completely unamazed. Sustained by faith in technology, floating through a dream.

There was a long room at the back of the museum, and he overheard a tour guide explaining the giant cases. It was a row of coffins. Each was an elaborate work of art, and the smaller slotted into the larger until the final coffin was the size of a room and was placed in the earth and sealed up for eternity. But now eternity was dug up and cracked open, the mysteries of the death cult exposed. The tourists clicked their cameras, getting their money's worth, a bit of culture. Then they boarded their air-conditioned buses and went to souks that sold junk.

He wandered through the rows of exhumed objects, objects which either from utility or beauty spoke clearly of life, and he could not shake the feeling of being in someone else's dream. Could they have dreamed forward, as we dreamed back to their lives? Could they have dreamt these people wandering heedless through their treasure?

A boy, five years old, wakes and tries to tell his father about pale ghosts drifting through the aisles of a vast temple, pointing at the Pharaoh's gold. The boy, rubbing his eyes, sits before a wooden bowl and the woman brings a pot and places it before them. The father scoops mashed beans into the boy's bowl. And then, Father, says the boy, they were looking at my bowl. The father smiles and passes his hand over the boy's head. He likes to watch him eat, and grow big. They begin their breakfast, as they do each morning, the sun rising above the fields, the Nile flowing tirelessly through the days.

They stopped before a painted wooden snake, projecting from a black box. A snake temple. The drawers, or doors, opened and the snake slid in or out on a wooden base. For exhibit, the snake poked out of doors.

'It's a cobra, Dad. Why is it in a box?'

'So it doesn't bite people.'

'If it escaped it would bite people. Wouldn't it?'

'That's the thing, with cobras.'

'Snakes can cause a really lot of trouble.'

'You're definitely in trouble if a cobra bites you.'

'What's definitely?'

'For sure.'

'Definitely in trouble. The snake told her to eat the apple, didn't he Dad? Then God took off his legs and said, Eat dust.'

They moved on, holding hands, between the glass cases. He told the boy lots of stories: myths and legends, Bible stories, invented-on-the-spot stories. Spider-Man and Batman and Jesus. Curious details caught the boy's interest. The expression 'eat dust', a fragment of scripture, like something from an action film. He had read the story to retell it to the boy and had discovered that the snake had originally had legs. God makes the snake limbless in punishment for tempting the people.

He had been struck, when he read, by another detail. In the story, God lies. God tells Adam and Eve that if they eat the fruit, or even touch it, they will die. The implication is that they will die on the spot. The snake explains that this is untrue: God does not want them to eat the fruit because then they will be able, like their Creator, to tell good from evil. Eve wishes to be wise, and eats the fruit. The snake has told the truth. She becomes wise. She understands that she is mortal.

God had lied as you would lie to children who have no way to comprehend what they are being warned against.

They passed a number of jars and cups, and stopped at the next interesting exhibit, a bow and set of arrows. The boy liked these toys. He liked knights and Vikings and now he liked Egyptians too, with their chariots and weapons. The father read the card and explained to the boy that the red pigment still visible on the tips of some of the arrowheads was poison.

'Snake poison, Dad.'

'Maybe. But there are other ways to get poison.'

The boy peered into the case. His mouth was open. This happened when he was thinking hard, but it also happened when he was tired. They had been looking around for nearly an hour and it was a sign that the boy would soon be harder to amuse. An hour is a long time when you are small and the days are so long you can get lost in them. The man decided they should skip the treasures of Tutankhamun. He imagined the boy's mother, breakfasted and relaxed, smiling when they returned from their journey.

'Why is the arrow like that, Dad?'

The arrows were barbed in order to rip the flesh badly if any attempt were made at extraction.

'To hurt more.'

'Oh.'

He mussed the boy's hair. 'Will we go now?'

The boy nodded. They headed for the stairs. They passed the entrance to the Mummy Room. He was not taking the boy to look at corpses. He could do without it himself, in fact. He remembered reading that Sadat had closed the exhibition because Islamists objected to the dead being displayed. Some fundamentalists had killed Sadat. The metro station in the square outside was named in his memory.

They stepped out into the light and stood on the steps. They could hear the traffic from the square.

'How about we sit down here on the steps and have a break. Then we'll go and get some ice cream.'

The boy did a little jump and landed bent-kneed, the weight of his body pulling his father's arm. They sat down.

They were just out of reach of the city. Many millions of people were out there. Charging through the streets in cars. Kneeling to pray. Walking home from a job, catching the smell of frying fish in a side street. Hustling for money, labouring in a factory or in a taxi, being a lift attendant, a street cleaner, a maker of felafel, an accountant, a shopkeeper, a shopkeeper's sweeper and mopper. Sprinkling parsley on your dinner. Buying trinkets for your room. Screaming when your team scored. Reading in the newspaper about a war in another country, while you had your hair cut. Watching the sun go down on the concrete skyline from an apartment on the seventh floor. Remembering when your son was born. Remembering when your wife was young.

Every generation went about its business, it seemed to him, as if none of it had ever happened before.

If people really saw that all their passions were infinitely ancient, he imagined, perhaps the traffic in the square would grind to a halt, the engines and horns go silent. The taxi drivers would sit in their cars with no reason to drive any further. Fares would say, 'Here is fine,' and would reach for wallets and remove the coloured notes. But the legal tender would be meaningless and would fall to the ground, and it would lie where it fell, and the passengers would get out, dazed, and wander like sleepwalkers through the stilled sea of vehicles. The drivers would fold their arms over the tops of the steering wheels, rest their chins on their arms, and gaze through their windshields.

He looked at his son. He was really alive, the realest thing there was. You could tell him to look both ways before he crossed the street, but about the other thing you could say nothing, because the other thing was just a story for him. The soldiers all fall down, then they get up and play another game.

He sat there for a moment with the boy, in the sunshine. It was good to enjoy the pleasant light of day.

'Let's get ice cream, Dad.'

'Let's go.'

They walked past the soldiers and police, back towards the noise of the city, the man and the boy, holding hands.

Notes on contributors

GREG BAXTER's essay 'Just Throwing Them Meat' appeared in *Dublin Review* 27 (Summer 2007).

BRIAN DILLON is the author of *In the Dark Room: A Journey in Memory*, which won the 2006 Irish Book Award for Non-fiction.

EDNA LONGLEY's edition of *The Annotated Collected Poems* of Edward Thomas is to be published in the spring.

JAKI McCARRICK's first play, *The Mushroom Pickers*, had its première at Southwark Playhouse in May 2006.

MOLLY MCCLOSKEY's most recent book is *Protection*, a novel

PHILIP Ó CEALLAIGH's first collection of stories, *Notes from a Turkish Whorehouse*, was awarded the Rooney Prize for Irish Literature and the Glen Dimplex New Writers Award for fiction.

IAN SANSOM may have something to do with *The Enthusiast Field Guide to Poetry*, which has just been published.

WILLIAM WALL's most book is *No Paradiso*, a collection of stories.

Just out from Dublin Review Books:

The Dublin Review Reader

Since the appearance of its first issue in December 2000, *The Dublin Review* has published new work by world-class writers four times a year. *The Dublin Review Reader* gathers a selection of the magazine's best non-fiction so far – essays of all kinds, reportage, criticism, travel writing and memoir.

With pieces by:

John Banville Angela Bourke Ciaran Carson
Amit Chaudhuri Catriona Crowe Brian Dillon
Anne Enright Roy Foster Vona Groarke
Selina Guinness Seamus Heaney Michael Hofmann
Ann Marie Hourihane Kathleen Jamie
Molly McCloskey Patrick McGrath Derek Mahon
Christina Hunt Mahony Lia Mills Andrew O'Hagan
Glenn Patterson Tim Robinson Ian Sansom
George Szirtes Colm Tóibín Maurice Walsh

352pp hardback, 215 x 136mm, ISBN 978-0-9556580-0-6

Available from good bookshops or via www.thedublinreview.com

subscribe to *the* Dublin Review

Four times a year, The Dublin Review *publishes first-rate critical and creative writing from Ireland and elsewhere, by writers such as John Banville, Angela Bourke, Ciaran Carson, Amit Chaudhuri, Brian Dillon, Terry Eagleton, Anne Enright, Roy Foster, Selina Guinness, Seamus Heaney, Michael Hofmann, Ann Marie Hourihane, Kathleen Jamie, Declan Kiberd, Edna Longley, Molly McCloskey, Patrick McGrath, Derek Mahon, Paul Muldoon, Dervla Murphy, Cees Nooteboom, George O'Brien, Andrew O'Hagan, Ruth Padel, Glenn Patterson, Tom Paulin, Tim Robinson, George Szirtes and Colm Tóibín.*

A year's subscription to The Dublin Review *brings four quarterly issues to your mailbox for the same low price you'd pay in a bookshop.* The Dublin Review *also makes an excellent gift.*

annual subscription rates:

Ireland & Britain
€30 / UK£24 for individuals; institutions add €12.70 / UK£10

Rest of world
€45 / US$60 for individuals; institutions add €12.70 / US$15

Payment by Visa / MC, or by cheque made payable to The Dublin Review. For credit card orders, please indicate billing address if different from postal address. Address order to The Dublin Review, P.O. Box 7948, Dublin 1, Ireland. **Or use the secure-ordering facility on our website: www.thedublinreview.com.**